101 Yummy Molasses Recipes

(101 Yummy Molasses Recipes - Volume 1)

Kelly Dill

Copyright: Published in the United States by Kelly Dill/ © KELLY DILL

Published on September, 22 2020

All rights reserved. No part of this publication may be reproduced, stored in retrieval system, copied in any form or by any means, electronic, mechanical, photocopying, recording or otherwise transmitted without written permission from the publisher. Please do not participate in or encourage piracy of this material in any way. You must not circulate this book in any format. KELLY DILL does not control or direct users' actions and is not responsible for the information or content shared, harm and/or actions of the book readers.

In accordance with the U.S. Copyright Act of 1976, the scanning, uploading and electronic sharing of any part of this book without the permission of the publisher constitute unlawful piracy and theft of the author's intellectual property. If you would like to use material from the book (other than just simply for reviewing the book), prior permission must be obtained by contacting the author at author@rutabagarecipes.com

Thank you for your support of the author's rights.

Content

101 AWESOME MOLASSES RECIPES 5

1. All American Turkey 5
2. Anadama Rolls With Mixed Seeds 5
3. Apple Gingerbread Cake With Cream 6
4. Apple Strudel Turnovers................... 7
5. Autumn Farmers' Market Salad 8
6. Bacon Fat Gingersnaps 9
7. Bacon Molasses Breakfast Sausage 10
8. Baked Yams With Ginger Molasses Butter 10
9. Barbecue Bean Soup 11
10. Barbecue Chicken Wings 11
11. Barbecued Baked Beans 12
12. Barbecued Beef Ribs With Molasses Bourbon Sauce 12
13. Blueberry Gingerbread Pancakes 13
14. Bourbon Molasses Ice Cream 14
15. Bourbon Molasses Chicken Drumsticks ... 14
16. Brown Bread 15
17. Bubby's Granola 15
18. Childhood Gingerbread With Molasses 16
19. Chipotle Cherry Barbecue Sauce 17
20. Chocolate Pecan Sheet Pie With Molasses 17
21. Christmas Gingerbread Cake With Maple Whipped Cream 19
22. Coffee Fruitcake 19
23. Colin Perry's Sorghum And Apple Sticky Pudding 20
24. Crystallized Ginger Spice Bars 21
25. Cumin Scented Eggplant With Pomegranate And Cilantro 22
26. Currant And Molasses Spice Cookies 22
27. Dark Ginger Rye Cake With Yogurt And Honey 23
28. Giant Pumpkin Muffins With Molasses Ginger Glaze 24
29. Ginger Date Muffins 24
30. Ginger Molasses Lace Cookies 25
31. Ginger Molasses Cake 25
32. Ginger Spice Cookies 26
33. Gingerbread Bars 26
34. Gingerbread Cake 27
35. Gingerbread Candy Canes 28
36. Gingerbread Layer Cake With Cream Cheese Frosting And Candied Pistachios............28
37. Gingerbread With Crystallized Ginger 29
38. Gingerbread With Vanilla Ice Cream And Exotic Caramel Sauce 30
39. Gingersnaps...31
40. Grilled Corn On The Cob With Chipotle, Molasses, And Orange Glaze 31
41. Grilled Molasses And Rum Glazed Fresh Ham 32
42. Grilled Pork Tenderloin With Molasses And Mustard..32
43. Guinness Stout Ginger Cake 33
44. Hot Molasses Milk Punch 34
45. Indian Corn Bread Pudding......................34
46. Indian Pudding.......................................34
47. Indian Pudding With Nutmeg Ice Cream .35
48. Individual Ginger Cakes With Apricot Sticky Sauce..36
49. Johnnycake Bread...................................36
50. Kentucky Gingerbread 37
51. Lamb Köfte With Yogurt Sauce And Muhammara..38
52. Lemon Molasses Chess Pie......................38
53. Lemon, Blueberry, And Gingerbread Trifles 39
54. Licorice Pudding.....................................40
55. Lime Molasses Vinaigrette 41
56. Molasses Barbecue Sauce 41
57. Molasses Crinkles 42
58. Molasses Ice Cream................................42
59. Molasses And Oat Soda Bread................42
60. Molasses, Rum, And Ginger Milk Punch ..43
61. Molasses Baked Onions 43
62. Molasses Brined Turkey With Gingersnap Gravy..44
63. Molasses Cured Pork Shoulder Bacon......45
64. Molasses And Buttermilk Gingerbread Squares...46
65. Moravian Crisps With Royal Icing 46
66. Muscovy Duck Breasts With Pomegranate Wine Sauce..47
67. Oatmeal And Prune Muffins 48
68. Old Fashioned Gingerbread 49
69. Old Fashioned Gingerbread With Molasses Whipped Cream 49
70. Orange Molasses Bread 50

71. Peter Luger Style Steak Sauce 50
72. Pineapple Upside Down Pumpkin Gingerbread 51
73. Pomegranate Cumin Dressing 52
74. Prune Armagnac Gingerbread 52
75. Pumpkin, Ginger And Molasses Tart 53
76. Raisin Ginger Breads 54
77. Real Gingerbread 54
78. Rich And Sticky Gingerbread With Marmalade 55
79. Scandinavian Spiced Christmas Cake With Applesauce Filling 55
80. Sherry Vinegar And Molasses Glazed Carrots 56
81. Smoky Bean Salad With Molasses Dressing 57
82. Soft Ginger Cookies 57
83. Sour Cream Bran Muffins 58
84. Speculoos Buttons 58
85. Spice Cookies 59
86. Spiced Pumpkin Pie 60
87. Spiced And Glazed Molasses Cookies 60
88. Sticky Sweet Grilled Pork Shoulder With Hoisin And Molasses 61
89. Stout Spice Cake With Lemon Glaze 62
90. Strawberries With Molasses Sour Cream Sauce 63
91. Striped Bass With Swiss Chard, Chestnuts, And Pomegranate Vinaigrette 63
92. Sweet And Spicy Chipotle Glazed Ribs 64
93. Three Nut Pie With Cranberries 64
94. Treacle Farls 65
95. Vanilla Ice Cream And Ginger Molasses Cookie Sandwiches 66
96. Whipped Sweet Potatoes With Nutmeg And Lemon 66
97. Whole Egg Molasses Buttercream 67
98. Whole Wheat Bran Bread Risney Manning 67
99. Whole Wheat Bread Hayes 68
100. Winterfell Black Bread 68
101. Yankee Oatmeal Molasses Bread 69

INDEX 71

CONCLUSION 73

101 Awesome Molasses Recipes

***

1. All American Turkey

Serving: makes 16 servings | Prep: | Ready in:

Ingredients

- Giblets and neck from the turkey
- 1 cup extra giblets
- 3 1/2 cups chicken broth
- 1 turkey (18 pounds), rinsed
- 1 orange, halved
- Paprika, to taste
- Salt and pepper, to taste
- Harvest Stuffing
- 6 tablespoons softened butter
- Pan juices from the turkey
- 1/4 cup butter
- 1/4 cup flour
- 2 tablespoons dry sherry
- 1 teaspoon dark molasses
- 1 teaspoon dried thyme
- Salt and freshly ground black pepper, to taste
- 1 tablespoon chopped sage Giblet mixture (see Step 1)

Direction

- Make Giblet Broth 1 day in advance: let the broth ingredients simmer for an hour till giblets are soft, skimming off any froth. Filter broth and reserve; set giblets and neck aside. Mince giblets and shred meat from neck; mix. Put a cover and chill broth and meats till ready to use.
- Preheat the oven to 325°F. Inside turkey body and the neck-cavities, squeeze orange halves; scatter with pepper, salt, and paprika. With stuffing, loosely fill cavities, with approximately 8 cups for body and 3 cups for neck. Truss turkey. Massage with softened butter and scatter pepper, salt and paprika over.
- On a rack in a roasting pan, put the turkey, breast-side facing up. Into the base of pan, add 2 cups of reserved Giblet Broth and loosely cover turkey using foil. Put in oven and allow to roast for 1 1/2 hours.
- Take off foil and let the turkey roast for 2 1/2 hours longer, basting with pan juices every 30 minutes.
- Increase oven temperature to 350°F and allow to cook for 1 to 1 1/4 hours longer, or till a thermometer pricked into the chunkiest part of thigh registers 180°F. The breast thickest part temperature should be 160°F. Once thigh is inserted with a small knife, the juices should run clear.
- For gravy: in a roasting pan, heat the pan juices, scratching up every brown bits. Defat; put into a measuring cup.
- In a saucepan, liquify the butter over moderate heat. Mix in flour and keep mixing till mixture browns lightly or for 2 to 3 minutes. Gradually add in 2 cups of reserved pan juices, mixing continuously till smooth. Boil, lower the heat to moderately-low and put the rest of the ingredients. Allow to simmer for 10 minutes, mixing, till gravy has thickened. Put additional broth for a thinner gravy. Fix seasonings; heat prior to serving.

Nutrition Information

2. Anadama Rolls With Mixed Seeds

Serving: Makes 16 rolls | Prep: | Ready in:

Ingredients

- 1 1/2 cups milk (do not use low-fat or non-fat)
- 1/3 cup mild-flavored (light) molasses
- 2 tablespoons (1/4 stick) unsalted butter
- 2 teaspoons salt
- 1/4 cup warm water (105°F to 115°F)
- 2 envelopes dry yeast
- 3/4 cup yellow cornmeal
- 1 1/2 cups whole wheat flour
- 2 3/4 cups (about) bread flour
- Additional yellow cornmeal
- 1 egg, beaten to blend (glaze)
- Assorted seeds (such as fennel, anise, celery and/or caraway)

Direction

- In a small saucepan, combine salt, butter, molasses and milk. Simmer. Into a heavy-duty mixer bowl fitted with paddle attachment, put the milk mixture. Allow to cool for 30 minutes to 155°F.
- Meantime, in a measuring cup, put quarter-cup of warm water. Scatter the yeast on top and mix to incorporate. Allow to sit till yeast melts into the milk mixture. Add in 3/4 cup of cornmeal. Add in the whole wheat flour. Add in sufficient bread flour, half cup at a time to create a slightly sticky dough. Transfer dough onto a floured area. Knead for 8 minutes till pliable and smooth, putting additional bread flour incase dough is very sticky. Shape the dough into round.
- Butter a big bowl. In a bowl, put the dough; flip to coat. Using plastic wrap, cover the bowl, then the towel. Allow the dough to rise for 1 1/2 hours in a warm area till doubled in volume.
- Scatter a liberal amount of cornmeal over 2 heavy big baking sheets. Punch dough down. Transfer onto floured area and knead for 3 minutes till smooth. Split the dough into 16 even pieces. Roll every piece among palms and work area into 8-inch lengthy rope approximately 3/4-inch thick. Holding a rope at each end, bind into loose knot. Redo with the rest of the ropes. Set on prepped baking sheets, place 2-inch away. Cover using the towels. Allow to rise in warm place for 45 minutes till doubled in size.
- Place a rack in middle and another rack in the top third of the oven and preheat to 375°F. With the egg glaze, brush the rolls. Scatter seeds over. Allow to bake for 20 minutes till rolls turn golden and sound empty once tapped, changing and turning around baking sheets midway through baking. Put the rolls to racks. Can be prepared for 2 weeks in advance. Allow to cool. Wrap with foil; let freeze. If wished, reheat the thawed wrapped rolls for 10 minutes in 350°F oven. Serve at room temperature or while warm.

Nutrition Information

- Calories: 204
- Total Fat: 3 g(5%)
- Saturated Fat: 2 g(8%)
- Sodium: 189 mg(8%)
- Fiber: 2 g(9%)
- Total Carbohydrate: 38 g(13%)
- Cholesterol: 16 mg(5%)
- Protein: 6 g(13%)

3. Apple Gingerbread Cake With Cream

Serving: Serves 10 | Prep: | Ready in:

Ingredients

- 3 tablespoons plus 1/2 cup unsalted butter, plus more for pan
- 1 cup (packed) light brown sugar, divided
- 1 pound lady apples, unpeeled, very thinly sliced, seeds removed, divided
- 2 cups all-purpose flour
- 1 1/2 teaspoons baking powder
- 1 1/2 teaspoons kosher salt
- 1 1/2 teaspoons ground cinnamon

- 1/2 teaspoon ground cloves
- 1/2 teaspoon ground nutmeg
- 1/2 cup robust-flavored (dark) molasses
- 1/2 cup pure maple syrup
- 2 large eggs, room temperature
- 2 tablespoons finely grated peeled ginger
- 1 1/2 teaspoons baking soda
- 1/2 cup heavy cream, plus more for serving
- A 10-inch springform pan

Direction

- Preheat the oven to 350°F. Grease the pan with butter and with a parchment round, line the base; butter the parchment. In a big skillet over moderate heat, heat 2 tablespoon water, 1/2 cup brown sugar and 1 tablespoon butter, mixing continuously, till butter is liquified and sugar is dissolved. Allow to cook for 2 minutes, avoid mixing instead swirl the skillet frequently, till big bubbles that are slow to burst create. Into the prepped pan, put the caramel and tilt the pan to equally coat the base.
- In the same skillet, liquefy a tablespoon of butter over moderate heat; put 1/2 of apples and separate by tossing. Let cook for 4 minutes, tossing frequently, till apples becomes tender and nearly translucent. Redo in exactly the same manner with one more tablespoon of butter and the rest of the apples. Allow the apples to rest till cool enough to touch, then set on top of caramel in a few overlapping layers. Reserve pan.
- In a big bowl, mix nutmeg, cloves, cinnamon, salt, baking powder and flour to blend; reserve. In a heatproof bowl place on top of a saucepan of barely simmering water, heat the remaining 1/2 cup butter, the remaining 1/2 cup brown sugar, maple syrup and molasses, mixing continuously, till mixture is smooth and butter is liquefied. Mix in the ginger and eggs. In a small bowl, mix the baking soda into quarter-cup of extremely hot water till dissolved, then mix into the molasses mixture. Into the reserved dry ingredients, mix the molasses mixture and scrape the batter on top of the apples, scattering equally. Equally sprinkle half cup of cream on top of batter.
- On a rimmed baking sheet lined with foil, put the cake and let bake for 35 to 45 minutes till middle is firm to the touch and a cake tester pricked into the middle comes out clean. To a wire rack, put the pan and allow the cake to cool in pan for 15 minutes. To loosen, trace a paring knife around the sides of cake, then take off sides of the pan and flip the cake onto rack. Cautiously take pan off and remove parchment, work gently for apples might adhere. Allow to cool fully.
- Cut the cake into wedges and serve drizzled with additional cream.
- Cake can be baked a day in advance. Keep securely covered at room temperature. In a microwave, rewarm the cake slightly and glaze top with maple syrup to revive the apples.

Nutrition Information

- Calories: 458
- Cholesterol: 87 mg(29%)
- Protein: 4 g(9%)
- Total Fat: 18 g(28%)
- Saturated Fat: 11 g(56%)
- Sodium: 385 mg(16%)
- Fiber: 2 g(8%)
- Total Carbohydrate: 71 g(24%)

4. Apple Strudel Turnovers

Serving: Makes 8 to 10 servings | Prep: | Ready in:

Ingredients

- 2 1/4 pounds Braeburn or Fuji apples (about 6 medium), peeled, cored, cut into 1/2-inch cubes
- 1/3 cup fresh lemon juice
- 1 cup sugar
- 1 teaspoon ground cinnamon

- 1/2 teaspoon ground ginger
- 1/4 teaspoon ground white pepper
- 1 1/4 cups (2 1/2 sticks) unsalted butter
- 1/3 cup water
- 2 tablespoons (packed) golden brown sugar
- 2 tablespoons mild-flavored (light) molasses
- 28 13x9-inch fresh phyllo pastry sheets or frozen, thawed (about 3/4 pound)
- 1 1/4 cups lightly toasted fresh breadcrumbs
- Vanilla ice cream

Direction

- In medium bowl, combine lemon juice and apple cubes. In small bowl, combine white pepper, ginger, cinnamon and 1 cup sugar to incorporate. In heavy big skillet over moderately-high heat, liquify quarter cup butter and mix continuously for 3 minutes till butter browns. Put in 1/3 cup of water, then the sugar mixture and cook for 4 minutes till syrup becomes deep amber color, mixing continuously. Stir in the brown sugar and mix till melted. Put in lemon juice and apple cubes; cook for 13 minutes till juices are thick and spoon leaves path once drawn across bottom of pan. Put in molasses and mix to incorporate. Distribute apple mixture evenly into 2 14-cube ice-cube trays. Freeze for a minimum of 4 hours till frozen. Frozen apple cubes can be made a month in advance. Put on a cover; keep frozen.
- In heavy small saucepan, liquify leftover 1 cup butter over moderately-low heat. On work surface, pile 14 phyllo sheets. Trim phyllo stack to create rectangle of 13x8-inch in size. Halve pile lengthwise, creating 2 13x4-inch piles; put on top each other. Cover using plastic wrap, then wet kitchen towel. Redo with the leftover 14 phyllo sheets, creating another stack. On work surface, put a phyllo strip. Grease lightly with liquified butter. Scatter 1 teaspoon breadcrumbs on top. Put the second phyllo strip over top. Grease lightly with liquified butter; scatter 1 teaspoon breadcrumbs on top. From ice-cube tray, get a frozen apple cube; put the rest of the cubes back into freezer. On lower short end of prepped phyllo strip, put the frozen apple cube. To make bottom edge lines up with left side, turn the bottom right corner of the strip over apple cube. Keep folding up the phyllo, flag-style, making triangle and sealing apple cube. With liquified butter, brush the triangle; put on rimmed baking sheet and turn onto freezer. Redo with the rest of the apple cubes and pastry strips. Turnovers can be prepared 2 weeks in advance. Put on a cover; keep frozen.
- Preheat the oven to 400°F. Bake the strudel turnovers on rimmed baking sheets for 13 minutes till golden brown. Serve strudel turnovers while warm together with vanilla ice cream.

Nutrition Information

- Calories: 656
- Saturated Fat: 19 g(95%)
- Sodium: 338 mg(14%)
- Fiber: 4 g(18%)
- Total Carbohydrate: 87 g(29%)
- Cholesterol: 76 mg(25%)
- Protein: 6 g(12%)
- Total Fat: 32 g(50%)

5. Autumn Farmers' Market Salad

Serving: Makes 6 servings | Prep: | Ready in:

Ingredients

- 4 1/2 to 5 cups 1/2-inch cubes peeled seeded butternut squash (from about one 2-pound squash)
- 2 tablespoons extra-virgin olive oil
- Pinch of dried crushed red pepper
- Coarse kosher salt
- 2 tablespoons orange juice
- 1 1/2 tablespoons walnut oil or other nut oil
- 1 1/2 teaspoons fresh lemon juice
- 4 ounces arugula (about 8 cups lightly packed)

- 1/2 cup walnuts, toasted, coarsely chopped
- 1/2 cup pomegranate seeds
- 2 teaspoons pomegranate molasses*

Direction

- Set the oven to 450°F for preheating. Toss the olive oil, crushed red pepper, and squash onto the large rimmed baking sheet. Sprinkle the mixture with coarse salt. Roast for 15 minutes. Flip the squash over with the spatula. Roast for 15 more minutes until the squash is tender and the edges are browned. Sprinkle with coarse salt. Take note that this can be prepared 2 hours ahead. Allow it to stand at room temperature.
- In a large shallow bowl, mix the walnut oil, lemon juice, and orange juice. Season the mixture with salt and pepper to taste. Add the pomegranate seeds, arugula, and walnuts. Toss the mixture well to coat. Season it with coarse salt and pepper to taste. Place the warm or room temperature squash over the salad. Before serving, drizzle it with pomegranate molasses.
- Note: The thick pomegranate syrup can be purchased online, supermarkets, and some Middle Eastern markets.

Nutrition Information

- Calories: 162
- Total Fat: 10 g(15%)
- Saturated Fat: 1 g(5%)
- Sodium: 380 mg(16%)
- Fiber: 3 g(13%)
- Total Carbohydrate: 19 g(6%)
- Protein: 2 g(4%)

6. Bacon Fat Gingersnaps

Serving: Makes 3 to 4 dozen cookies | Prep: | Ready in:

Ingredients

- 3/4 cup bacon fat (from 1 1/2 to 2 pounds bacon), at room temperature
- 1 cup sugar, plus 1/4 cup for rolling
- 1/4 cup molasses (not blackstrap) or cane syrup, such as Steen's or Lyle's
- 1 large egg
- 2 cups all-purpose flour
- 1 1/2 teaspoons kosher salt
- 2 teaspoons baking soda
- 2 teaspoons ground ginger
- 1/2 teaspoon ground cloves
- 1/2 teaspoon ground cinnamon

Direction

- In a food processor, mix every ingredient, and pulse till creating a smooth, stiff dough. Wrap dough with plastic and chill in refrigerator for several hours.
- Preheat an oven to 350°. With parchment paper, line the 2 baking sheets.
- In a shallow bowl, put quarter cup sugar. Breaking off a-tablespoon lumps, roll dough into balls, drop into sugar, turn to coat, and on the baking sheets, set balls 2 inches apart.
- Bake for 10 to 12 minutes, till cookies are deep brown. Allow to cool for several minutes on baking sheets, then turn onto a rack to cool fully.

Nutrition Information

- Calories: 85
- Saturated Fat: 1 g(7%)
- Sodium: 69 mg(3%)
- Fiber: 0 g(1%)
- Total Carbohydrate: 12 g(4%)
- Cholesterol: 8 mg(3%)
- Protein: 1 g(2%)
- Total Fat: 4 g(6%)

7. Bacon Molasses Breakfast Sausage

Serving: Makes 1 1/2 cups; Serves 4 to 6 | Prep: | Ready in:

Ingredients

- 8 ounces ground pork
- 4 ounces bacon, finely chopped
- 1 teaspoon molasses
- 1 teaspoon smoked paprika (pimentón)
- 1/2 teaspoon brown sugar
- 1/2 teaspoon kosher salt
- 1/4 teaspoon dried sage
- 1/4 teaspoon black pepper

Direction

- Mix together the black pepper, sage, salt, brown sugar, smoked paprika, molasses, bacon and pork till well blended.
- Over moderate heat, heat a skillet and cook a small spoonful of sausage for a couple of minutes per side. Taste and modify the seasonings, if needed.
- When pleased with the balance of flavor, chill the mixture for 1 hour to incorporate the flavors. For the sausage, shape it into 1/4-inch-thick and 2-inch-wide patties and fry over moderately-high heat for 5 minutes per side till crisp and brown.
- The uncooked sausage can be kept in refrigerator for 1 week, or in freezer for 3 months.

Nutrition Information

- Calories: 276
- Sodium: 221 mg(9%)
- Fiber: 0 g(1%)
- Total Carbohydrate: 2 g(1%)
- Cholesterol: 60 mg(20%)
- Protein: 13 g(27%)
- Total Fat: 23 g(36%)
- Saturated Fat: 8 g(41%)

8. Baked Yams With Ginger Molasses Butter

Serving: Makes 6 servings | Prep: | Ready in:

Ingredients

- 1/2 cup (1 stick) unsalted butter, room temperature
- 3 tablespoons (packed) golden brown sugar
- 1 tablespoon mild-flavored (light) molasses
- 1/2 teaspoon ground ginger
- 1/4 teaspoon ground cinnamon
- Pinch of ground cloves
- 3 tablespoons minced crystallized ginger
- 6 8-ounce yams (red-skinned sweet potatoes), rinsed, patted dry

Direction

- In small bowl, combine the initial 6 ingredients to incorporate. Mix in the crystallized ginger. Put salt and liberal amount of pepper to season. Can be done 3 days in advance. Put a cover; refrigerate. Bring the ginger-molasses butter to room temperature prior to using.
- Preheat an oven to 350°F. Using fork, prick yams in few areas. Allow to bake on rimmed baking sheet for 50 minutes till soft when pricked with fork.
- Slit each yam lengthwise and push in ends to reveal top. Into every yam, scoop 2 tablespoons of ginger-molasses butter and serve.

Nutrition Information

- Calories: 427
- Saturated Fat: 10 g(49%)
- Sodium: 30 mg(1%)
- Fiber: 8 g(33%)
- Total Carbohydrate: 70 g(23%)
- Cholesterol: 41 mg(14%)
- Protein: 3 g(6%)
- Total Fat: 16 g(24%)

9. Barbecue Bean Soup

Serving: Makes about 13 cups, serving 8 | Prep: | Ready in:

Ingredients

- 3 cups chopped onion
- 3 garlic cloves, minced
- 1/4 cup vegetable oil
- 2 tablespoons chili powder
- 2 tablespoons ground cumin
- 1 teaspoon ground allspice
- 1/4 teaspoon ground cloves
- two 32-ounce cans tomatoes including the juice, chopped
- three 16-ounce cans pink beans or pinto beans, drained and rinsed
- two 7-ounce bottles roasted red peppers, rinsed, drained, and chopped
- 3 1/2 cups beef broth
- 1/4 cup molasses
- 1 tablespoon Tabasco
- 2 teaspoons cider vinegar, or to taste

Direction

- Cook garlic and onion in oil in a kettle on medium heat till onion is soft, mixing. Mix in cloves, allspice, cumin and chili powder; simmer for 1 minute. Add pepper and salt to taste, Tabasco, molasses, broth, beans, roasted peppers, and tomatoes with juice; simmer soup for 1 1/2 hours, occasionally mixing, partially covered. Mix vinegar into soup; simmer soup till heated through. You can make soup 2 days ahead, fully cooled, uncovered then kept covered and chilled. Reheat soup; put in thermoses.

Nutrition Information

- Calories: 334
- Fiber: 15 g(59%)
- Total Carbohydrate: 54 g(18%)
- Protein: 13 g(27%)
- Total Fat: 9 g(15%)
- Saturated Fat: 1 g(5%)
- Sodium: 1003 mg(42%)

10. Barbecue Chicken Wings

Serving: Makes 60 pieces | Prep: | Ready in:

Ingredients

- 2 cups ketchup
- 1/2 cup cider vinegar
- 1/2 cup water
- Juice of 1 lemon
- 2 tablespoons Worcestershire sauce
- 2 tablespoons Tabasco sauce
- 2 tablespoons unsulfured molasses
- 2 tablespoons Dijon mustard
- 2 tablespoons chili powder
- 1/4 cup (packed) dark brown sugar
- 2 teaspoons finely minced garlic
- 2 teaspoons smoked paprika
- Salt and freshly ground black pepper, to taste
- 30 chicken wings (tips removed), rinsed and patted dry
- 4 scallions, thinly sliced on the diagonal, for garnish

Direction

- Prepare the barbecue sauce in advance: in a heavy saucepan, mix every sauce ingredient. Cook over moderately-low heat for 10 to 12 minutes, mixing, to heat through and to incorporate the flavors. Keep from boiling. Filter to get rid of the garlic. Allow to cool to room temperature. This will make 3 cups. Use right away or chill with a cover for up to 2 weeks.
- Preheat an oven to 350°F.
- Part chicken wings at joint with a sharp knife. Reserve.

- In a big bowl, put the chicken portions and toss thoroughly with 1 1/2 cups of sauce. On 2 or 3 baking sheets, arrange the portions in 1 layer, prevent overcrowding them. Bake for 45 to 50 minutes, basting one or two times with more sauce. Put the wings on platter and scatter scallions over the top.

Nutrition Information

11. Barbecued Baked Beans

Serving: Serves 6 to 8 | Prep: | Ready in:

Ingredients

- 1 pound California small white beans
- 1/2 cup onions, finely chopped
- 1/2 cup celery with leaves, finely chopped
- 1/4 cup green bell pepper, chopped
- 1 tablespoon garlic, minced
- 3 tablespoons olive oil
- 1 16-ounce can tomato sauce or 6 large fresh tomatoes chopped and stewed for 1hour
- 1/4 cup dark brown sugar
- 1/4 cup thick molasses
- 1 tablespoon dry mustard
- 3 tablespoons Worcestershire sauce
- 1/2 teaspoon ground cloves
- chicken, veal, or pork stock (optional)
- 2 bay leaves
- 1 teaspoon salt
- 1 teaspoon cracked black pepper
- 1 teaspoon fresh thyme
- 1 cup country cured slab bacon, diced

Direction

- Wash beans; put in a big pot. Cover using cool water; boil it for 5 minutes. Take off heat; sit with tight lid for 1 hour. Sauté garlic, bell pepper, celery and onions in olive oil for 4 minutes on high heat in a cast iron skillet or till onion is translucent. Add cloves, Worcestershire sauce, mustard, molasses, sugar and tomato sauce; simmer for 30 minutes. Pour water from beans off; replace using 3 1/2 cups meat stock or fresh cool water. Add thyme, pepper, salt and bay leaves; simmer till beans are tender, covered. Sauté bacon cubes then drain. Drain bean liquids; put aside. Mix tomato sauce and beans in a bean pot or Dutch oven; put bacon over. Bake for 3-5 hours in 300° oven. Mix beans occasionally; as needed, add reserved liquid.

Nutrition Information

- Calories: 438
- Protein: 20 g(40%)
- Total Fat: 10 g(15%)
- Saturated Fat: 2 g(9%)
- Sodium: 518 mg(22%)
- Fiber: 14 g(54%)
- Total Carbohydrate: 71 g(24%)
- Cholesterol: 3 mg(1%)

12. Barbecued Beef Ribs With Molasses Bourbon Sauce

Serving: Makes 6 servings | Prep: | Ready in:

Ingredients

- 1 1/2 cups water
- 1 12-ounce bottle pale ale
- 1/4 cup mild-flavored (light) molasses
- 5 fresh thyme sprigs
- 1 tablespoon sugar
- 1 tablespoon salt
- 1 bay leaf
- 1/2 teaspoon ground white pepper
- 16 beef short ribs or 8 whole beef ribs
- 1 tablespoon vegetable oil
- 1 small onion, finely chopped
- 1 cup red wine vinegar
- 2 cups ketchup

- 1/2 cup mild-flavored (light) molasses
- 1/4 cup water
- 1/2 cup bourbon
- 1 1/2 teaspoons salt
- 1/2 teaspoon ground white pepper
- Leaves from 5 fresh thyme sprigs
- Charcoal chimney
- 45 charcoal briquettes

Direction

- Marinade and ribs: in a heavy medium saucepan, mix every ingredient excluding ribs. Boil. Let the marinade cool fully. In a big resealable heavy-duty plastic bag, put the ribs; put the marinade. Enclose the bag; flip to cover the ribs. Chill overnight, flipping bag from time to time.
- Sauce: in a heavy big saucepan, heat the oil over moderately-high heat. Put the onion and sauté for 6 minutes till golden brown. Put the vinegar and let boil for 5 minutes till mixture reduces to 3/4 cup. Take off heat. Put the 1/4 cup water, molasses and ketchup, then the bourbon; mix to incorporate. Simmer the sauce. Mix in the white pepper and salt. Allow to simmer for 10 minutes to incorporate the flavors. Mix in the thyme leaves. Sauce can be made a day in advance. Put a cover and chill.
- In the base of the charcoal chimney, put a handful of torn newspaper. Place 30 charcoal briquettes on top. Take top grill rack off barbecue. Set the chimney on the bottom rack. Light the newspaper; allow the charcoal to burn for 30 minutes till ash is gray.
- Unlatch base barbecue vent. Onto 1 side of the base rack, transfer hot charcoal. Move charcoal to cover about 1/3 of rack at 1 side with metal spatula. With water, fill foil loaf pan midway; on the base rack, put opposite charcoal.
- Put top rack back to barbecue. On top rack above water, set the ribs in loaf pan. Cover barbecue using the lid, placing top vent right on top of the ribs. Through the top vent, insert the stem of a candy thermometer, with tip close the ribs and gauge outside, prevent the thermometer from touching neither the meat nor barbecue rack; while cooking, retain the thermometer in place. To retain temperature between 250°F to 300°F use bottom and top vents, opening the vents wider to raise the heat and closing to reduce the heat. Retain other vents unopened. Monitor the temperature every 10 minutes.
- Let the ribs cook for 3 hours in all till meat is really soft once pricked with knife, flipping ribs from time to time and basting frequently with the sauce on the final 10 minutes of cooking. Open barbecue just if needed to baste or flip meat and close immediately to lessen loss of smoke and heat.
- After the initial 30 minutes of cooking, use the exactly the same technique earlier to light 15 more charcoal briquettes in charcoal chimney place over non-flammable area. Lift off top rack with ribs using oven mitts and set on heatproof area incase cooking temperature goes down to below 250°F. To the bottom rack, put 1/2 of hot gray charcoal from chimney with tongs. Put top rack back on the barbecue, setting ribs in loaf pan on top of water. Place the lid to cover.
- Put the ribs to plates; brush with additional sauce and serve, separately passing any leftover sauce.

Nutrition Information

---

13. Blueberry Gingerbread Pancakes

Serving: Makes about 16 | Prep: | Ready in:

Ingredients

- 2 cups unbleached all purpose flour
- 1 1/2 teaspoons baking powder
- 1 1/4 teaspoons ground ginger
- 3/4 teaspoon pumpkin pie spice
- 1/4 teaspoon baking soda

- 1/4 teaspoon salt
- 3/4 cup mild-flavored (light) molasses
- 3/4 cup buttermilk
- 2 large eggs
- 3 tablespoons vegetable oil
- 2 cups fresh blueberries or frozen (unthawed)
- Additional vegetable oil

Direction

- Preheat the oven to 200°F. Into medium bowl, sift the initial 6 ingredients 2 times. In a big bowl, beat 3 tablespoons oil, eggs, buttermilk and molasses to incorporate. Put the dry ingredients and beat the mixture till smooth. Fold into the blueberries.
- Over moderately-low heat, heat a big nonstick skillet. With more oil, brush the skillet liberally. Into skillet, drop 3 tablespoons of batter for every pancake, do it in batches. Scatter every pancake into 3-inch round with the back of spoon. Let cook for 1 1/2 minutes till bottoms are slight golden brown. Flip pancakes over and allow to cook for 1 1/2 minutes till just cooked completely. Turn pancakes onto baking sheet; retain warmth in the oven for up to 20 minutes. With more oil, brush skillet for every batch.

Nutrition Information

- Calories: 159
- Total Carbohydrate: 27 g(9%)
- Cholesterol: 24 mg(8%)
- Protein: 3 g(6%)
- Total Fat: 5 g(7%)
- Saturated Fat: 1 g(3%)
- Sodium: 127 mg(5%)
- Fiber: 1 g(4%)

14. Bourbon Molasses Ice Cream

Serving: Makes 1 pint | Prep: 10mins | Ready in:

Ingredients

- 2 tablespoons light molasses
- 1 tablespoon bourbon
- 1 pint vanilla ice cream, slightly softened

Direction

- Preparation Stir molasses and bourbon into slightly softened vanilla ice cream. Freeze ice cream until firm.

Nutrition Information

- Calories: 174
- Saturated Fat: 4 g(22%)
- Sodium: 57 mg(2%)
- Fiber: 0 g(2%)
- Total Carbohydrate: 23 g(8%)
- Cholesterol: 29 mg(10%)
- Protein: 2 g(5%)
- Total Fat: 7 g(11%)

15. Bourbon Molasses Chicken Drumsticks

Serving: Makes 4 servings | Prep: | Ready in:

Ingredients

- 1/4 cup (1/2 stick) butter
- 1 cup minced onion
- 1 cup ketchup
- 1/4 cup molasses
- 2 tablespoons (packed) brown sugar
- 1 1/2 tablespoons Worcestershire sauce
- 2 teaspoons yellow mustard
- 3/4 teaspoon ground black pepper, divided
- 1/4 teaspoon chili powder
- 1/4 cup bourbon
- 1 1/2 teaspoons coarse kosher salt
- 12 chicken drumsticks

Direction

- In a big saucepan, liquify butter over moderate heat. Put the onion; sauté for 6 minutes till tender. Put the following 5 ingredients, chili powder and quarter teaspoon pepper. Lower the heat to moderately-low; let simmer for 15 minutes till sauce thickens. Mix in bourbon; allow to cook for 3 minutes till heated completely. Put salt to season. Can be prepared a day in advance. Put a cover and refrigerate.
- In a bowl, combine 1/2 teaspoon pepper and 1 1/2 teaspoons salt. Detach drumsticks skin. Beneath the skin, massage pepper and salt mixture without breaking the skin. Place a cover; allow to sit for 30 minutes at room temperature.
- Have barbecue ready at moderate heat. Let the drumsticks grill for 25 minutes till juices run clear and skin is crisp, flipping to cook every side. To small bowl, put half cup barbecue sauce; set aside. Brush the drumsticks with the rest of the sauce and allow to cook for 3 minutes more till glaze creates. Put the drumsticks to a platter and serve along with the reserved sauce.

Nutrition Information

- Calories: 951
- Cholesterol: 398 mg(133%)
- Protein: 73 g(147%)
- Total Fat: 48 g(75%)
- Saturated Fat: 17 g(86%)
- Sodium: 1313 mg(55%)
- Fiber: 1 g(5%)
- Total Carbohydrate: 45 g(15%)

16. Brown Bread

Serving: 20 | Prep: 30mins | Ready in:

Ingredients

- 1 cup bread flour
- 1 cup whole wheat flour
- 1 cup cornmeal
- 1 cup molasses
- 2 cups water
- 1 teaspoon baking soda
- 1 teaspoon salt

Direction

- Mix together baking soda, cornmeal, whole wheat flour and bread flour in a big bowl. Mix in water and molasses; blend till incorporated. Into 2 slightly oiled coffee cans, put the batter, fill approximately 2/3 full.
- Into a steamer, set the loaves, place a cover and allow to steam over low heat. Let steam for an hour and 45 minutes, till loaves are firm.

Nutrition Information

- Calories: 93 calories;
- Protein: 1.3
- Total Fat: 0.3
- Sodium: 186
- Total Carbohydrate: 22.1
- Cholesterol: 0

17. Bubby's Granola

Serving: Serves 15 to 18 | Prep: | Ready in:

Ingredients

- 1/2 cup vegetable oil, plus more for the baking sheets
- 3/4 cup honey
- 1/3 cup molasses
- Pinch of kosher salt
- 2 pounds (10 cups) rolled oats
- 3/4 cup pecan pieces
- 3/4 cup walnut pieces
- 1/4 cup sesame seeds
- 1/3 cup pumpkin seeds
- 1/3 sunflower seeds

- 2 cups raisins

Direction

- Preheat an oven to 350°F. Slightly grease 2 baking sheets.
- In a small heavy saucepan, mix together the salt, molasses, honey and vegetable oil over low heat. Allow to cook for 1 to 2 minutes, or till well incorporated and extremely hot. Take the mixture away from heat.
- In a big bowl, mix sunflower seeds, pumpkin seeds, sesame seeds, walnuts, pecans and rolled oats.
- On top of oat mixture, put the honey mixture and toss quickly to blend. Ensure every seed, nut, and oat are well coated.
- On the prepped baking sheets, spread out the granola equally. Bake for approximately 30 minutes, mixing every 5 minutes or so, till golden, not deep, brown. Keep it from overbaking.
- Take the pans out of the oven and let the granola to cool fully. It will become crispy once it cools. In a big container with lid, put the granola. Tightly cover and keep at room temperature. Just prior to serving, put in the raisins.

Nutrition Information

- Calories: 464
- Total Fat: 18 g(27%)
- Saturated Fat: 2 g(9%)
- Sodium: 15 mg(1%)
- Fiber: 7 g(28%)
- Total Carbohydrate: 73 g(24%)
- Protein: 10 g(20%)

18. Childhood Gingerbread With Molasses

Serving: Makes one 8-inch square cake with a shiny, dark surface and a tender, aromatic crumb | Prep: | Ready in:

Ingredients

- 2 cups all-purpose flour
- 2 teaspoons baking powder
- 1 teaspoon cinnamon
- 1 teaspoon powdered ginger, or up to 2 teaspoons for a stronger ginger bite
- 1/2 teaspoon allspice
- 1 cup blackstrap molasses or dark molasses
- 1 cup boiling water
- 1/2 cup packed light brown sugar
- 8 tablespoons (1 stick) salted butter (if using unsalted butter, add 1/4 teaspoon salt to the dry ingredients), cut into small chunks, softened
- 2 large or extra-large eggs, at room temperature

Direction

- In the upper third of oven, set a rack and preheat the oven to about 365°F, set the dial midway along 350°F and 375°F. Liberally oil a square cake pan, 8-inch in size.
- In a medium bowl, mix the powdered spices, baking powder and flour, and combine thoroughly; reserve. Into a 2-cup measuring cup or more, put the molasses, pour boiling water, and mix to dissolve well. Reserve.
- In a big bowl, put the butter chunks and brown sugar and using a mixer or a wooden spoon to cream together. In a separate bowl, beat the eggs briskly, then mix them into butter-sugar mixture. Put approximately half-cup of flour mixture and beat or mix in on low speed, then put approximately the same amount of the warm molasses-water and mix. Keep adding flour alternating with liquid, mixing or beating briskly every time. Beat briskly after the last addition for batter will be quite liquid, then put into the prepped pan.
- Let bake for 25 minutes, then turn the heat to 350°F and allow to bake for 15 to 20 minutes more till finish and a skewer pricked into the middle comes out clean.

- Allow to cool in pan for 20 minutes or longer to let crumb set prior to serving. Serve right from the pan.

Nutrition Information

- Calories: 275
- Saturated Fat: 5 g(26%)
- Sodium: 149 mg(6%)
- Fiber: 1 g(3%)
- Total Carbohydrate: 46 g(15%)
- Cholesterol: 55 mg(18%)
- Protein: 3 g(7%)
- Total Fat: 9 g(14%)

19. Chipotle Cherry Barbecue Sauce

Serving: Makes about 2 cups | Prep: | Ready in:

Ingredients

- 1 cup ketchup
- 1/2 cup cherry preserves
- 2 tablespoons fresh lemon juice
- 2 tablespoons mild-flavored (light) molasses
- 2 tablespoons golden brown sugar
- 1 tablespoon Worcestershire sauce
- 1 tablespoon soy sauce
- 1 teaspoon finely grated lemon peel
- 1 to 2 canned chipotle chiles in adobo, minced, plus 1 tablespoon adobo sauce from can
- 1 teaspoon liquid smoke
- 1 teaspoon onion powder
- 1 teaspoon unsweetened cocoa powder
- Ingredient info: Chipotle chiles in adobo (a spicy tomato sauce) are available at some supermarkets and at specialty foods stores and Latin markets. Liquid smoke is a smoke-flavored liquid seasoning. Look for it at supermarkets and specialty foods stores.

Direction

- Simmer cocoa powder, onion powder, liquid smoke, adobo sauce, chiles, lemon peel, Worcestershire sauce, soy sauce, brown sugar, molasses, lemon juice, cherry preserves and ketchup in a medium saucepan, mixing often. Lower heat to medium low; simmer for 10 minutes, mixing often. Season sauce with pepper and salt to taste; you can make it 1 week ahead. Tightly cover; refrigerate.

Nutrition Information

- Calories: 234
- Fiber: 1 g(5%)
- Total Carbohydrate: 60 g(20%)
- Protein: 2 g(3%)
- Total Fat: 0 g(0%)
- Saturated Fat: 0 g(0%)
- Sodium: 1145 mg(48%)

20. Chocolate Pecan Sheet Pie With Molasses

Serving: Serves 20–24 | Prep: 1.5hours | Ready in:

Ingredients

- 3/4 cup pecans (about 2 ounces)
- 1 tablespoon plus 1 1/2 teaspoons granulated sugar
- 2 1/2 teaspoons kosher salt
- 4 1/2 cups all-purpose flour, plus more for surface
- 1 1/2 cups (3 sticks) chilled unsalted butter, cut into pieces
- 1 cup (2 sticks) unsalted butter
- 2 cups granulated sugar
- 1 2/3 cups light corn syrup
- 1/3 cup robust-flavored (dark) molasses (not blackstrap)
- 2 tablespoons fresh lemon juice
- 2 teaspoons vanilla extract
- 1 teaspoon kosher salt
- 8 large eggs, beaten to blend

- 1 large egg white
- 1/4 cup (packed) light brown sugar
- 1/2 teaspoon kosher salt
- 2 cups pecans (about 8 ounces)
- 1 tablespoon granulated sugar
- 8 ounces (about 1 1/2 cups) bittersweet chocolate, chopped, or chocolate chips
- 1/2 cup heavy cream
- An 18x13x1" rimmed baking sheet

Direction

- For the crust: in food processor, pulse salt, granulated sugar and pecans till finely ground. Put 4 1/2 cups of flour and pulse till incorporated. Put the butter and pulse till pea-size portions remain. Slowly stream in 3/4 cup of ice water with motor running; pulse till dough starts to create big clumps.
- Onto a work surface, transfer the dough. Knead briskly to blend, then press into flat rectangle. With plastic wrap, wrap the dough and refrigerate for an hour.
- Place a rack in middle of the oven; preheat the oven to 375°F. With parchment paper, line the baking sheet, retaining an overhang on two lengthy sides.
- Put the dough to a slightly floured, lengthy piece of parchment at a minimum of 20 inches and unroll to a bigger rectangle. Put one more floured piece of parchment on top; roll to a rectangle, 19x15-inch in size approximately quarter-inch thick, in case dough turns very warm, refrigerate for 5 minutes. Peel off top layer of parchment. To baking sheet, slowly put the dough lined with parchment to make parchment short sides hang on top of baking sheet short sides. Up the sides of the baking sheet, force the dough till dough is just hanging over the rim, then clip so the edges are flush. Flute using a fork, if wished, then puncture base of the dough using fork. Freeze the dough for 20 minutes.
- Let the crust bake for 15 to 20 minutes till edges are browned lightly and starting to set. To a wire rack, put the baking sheet and allow to cool.
- For the filling: in a big saucepan, liquify the butter over moderate heat. Let cook for 5 to 8 minutes, mixing from time to time, till butter smells nutty and solids start to brown. Take off heat and quickly mix in the granulated sugar. Put salt, vanilla, lemon juice, molasses and corn syrup and mix to incorporate. Put the eggs and beat till smooth.
- Pull out the middle rack of the oven; set the crust on rack. Into the crust, put the filling and cautiously put rack back to oven. Let the pie bake for 10 minutes. Lower the oven temperature to 325°F and keep baking for 20 to 25 minutes longer till filling is set yet wiggles slightly once baking sheet is knocked. To a wire rack, put the pan and allow to cool.
- For candied pecans: raise the oven temperature to 350°F. In a big bowl, beat the egg white till foamy. Put salt and brown sugar and beat to incorporate. Put the pecans and stir using a spoon till equally covered.
- On a rimmed baking sheet lined with foil, scatter the pecan mixture and allow to bake for 8 minutes, tossing one time midway through, till crisp and toasted. Toss the pecans, then put to a big bowl. Scatter granulated sugar on top and coat by tossing. Allow to cool, tossing from time to time to guarantee pecans don't adhere together, then roughly chop.
- For the chocolate ganache and finish the pie: in a small bowl, put the chocolate. In a small saucepan, simmer the cream, then put on top of chocolate. Knock the bowl to immerse the chocolate in cream; allow to sit for a minute.
- Mix chocolate mixture in the middle using a small whisk till smooth and shiny. Put ganache on top of pie and using an offset spatula, scatter equally. While chocolate is warm, scatter the candied pecans on top of pie. Allow the pie to cool at room temperature for a minimum of 2 hours or refrigerate for an hour.
- Put the tart to a big chopping board or serving platter using parchment. Slice into cubes to serve.

Nutrition Information

- Calories: 637
- Protein: 7 g(14%)
- Total Fat: 37 g(57%)
- Saturated Fat: 18 g(89%)
- Sodium: 359 mg(15%)
- Fiber: 3 g(10%)
- Total Carbohydrate: 74 g(25%)
- Cholesterol: 131 mg(44%)

21. Christmas Gingerbread Cake With Maple Whipped Cream

Serving: Serves 14 to 16 | Prep: | Ready in:

Ingredients

- Nonstick vegetable oil spray
- 3 cups all purpose flour
- 2 tablespoons ground ginger
- 2 teaspoons baking soda
- 1 1/4 teaspoons ground cinnamon
- 3/4 teaspoon ground cloves
- 1/2 teaspoon ground nutmeg
- 1/4 teaspoon salt
- 1/3 cup minced crystallized ginger
- 10 tablespoons (1 1/4 sticks) unsalted butter, room temperature
- 1 cup (packed) golden brown sugar
- 3 large eggs
- 1 cup mild-flavored (light) molasses
- 1 cup boiling water
- 2 1/2 teaspoons grated orange peel
- 3 cups chilled whipping cream
- 1/2 cup pure maple syrup
- 1 tablespoon finely chopped crystallized ginger
- Orange peel strips

Direction

- For cake: place the rack in middle of the oven and preheat the oven to 350°F. With nonstick spray, coat a cake pan 10-inch-diameter and 2-inch-high sides. Line parchment paper on bottom of the pan; grease the paper. Into medium bowl, sift the flour and following 6 ingredients. Add in the crystallized ginger.
- In a big bowl, beat butter using electric mixer till fluffy. Whisk in the brown sugar. Beat in the eggs one by one. Slowly whisk in the molasses, then a cup of boiling water. Add in the grated orange peel. Slowly stir in the dry ingredients.
- To prepped pan, put the batter. Let bake for an hour till tester pricked into middle of the cake comes out clean. Put the pan to rack and allow to cool for 15 minutes. Trace a knife around pan sides. Invert cake onto the rack; remove the paper. Allow to cool.
- For filling and frosting: in a big bowl, whisk maple syrup and cream till stiff peaks create.
- Slice the cake horizontally making 3 even layers. Put a layer of cake to platter, cut side facing up. Scatter 1 1/2 cups of whipped cream mixture on top. Redo the layering with another layer of cake and 1 1/2 cups of the whipped cream mixture. Place the leftover cake layer on top, cut side facing down. Scatter the rest of the whipped cream on sides and over the top of the cake. On top of cake around edge, scatter crystallized ginger. Jazz up with orange peel strips. Cover using cake dome; refrigerate for a minimum of 1 hour and a maximum of 6 hours.

Nutrition Information

22. Coffee Fruitcake

Serving: Makes 2 loaves | Prep: 25mins | Ready in:

Ingredients

- 3 1/2 cups plus 2 tablespoons all-purpose flour
- 2 teaspoons cinnamon

- 1 teaspoon salt
- 1 teaspoon ground cloves
- 1 teaspoon freshly grated nutmeg
- 1 lb dried currants (3 1/3 cups)
- 1 lb raisins (3 cups)
- 1 cup lukewarm strong coffee
- 1 teaspoon baking soda
- 2 sticks (1 cup) unsalted butter, softened
- 2 cups packed light brown sugar
- 4 large eggs
- 1 cup molasses (not robust or blackstrap)
- 2 (9- by 5- by 3-inch) loaf pans

Direction

- In center of oven, set the oven rack and preheat the oven to 250°F. With oil, slightly brush loaf pans, then line foil on the bottom and up the sides, patting corners to aid to stick.
- In a big bowl, sift together nutmeg, cloves, salt, cinnamon and flour.
- In a bowl, toss raisins and currants together with 2 tablespoons of the flour mixture. In a small bowl, mix together baking soda and coffee till dissolved.
- In a big bowl with electric mixer, beat together sugar and butter at moderately-high speed for 5 to 7 minutes till fluffy and light. Put in the eggs, 2 at a time, mixing thoroughly between additions, and mix in molasses. Lower the speed to low, then alternately put the flour mixture and coffee mixture in batches, starting and finishing with flour mixture and stirring till just smooth. Fold in the dried fruit mixture.
- Distribute the batter into loaf pans and lightly tap bottom of every pan against counter to level tops.
- Bake till a wooden pick or skewer pricked in the middle of each cake comes out clean for 2 3/4 to 3 1/4 hours, cakes may go down slightly in middle. Allow to cool pans on racks for 10 minutes, then using a knife, loosen foil from the sides of pans and invert cakes onto racks. Remove foil and cool cakes fully for 3 hours.

Nutrition Information

- Calories: 348
- Cholesterol: 47 mg(16%)
- Protein: 4 g(9%)
- Total Fat: 8 g(13%)
- Saturated Fat: 5 g(24%)
- Sodium: 174 mg(7%)
- Fiber: 3 g(10%)
- Total Carbohydrate: 68 g(23%)

23. Colin Perry's Sorghum And Apple Sticky Pudding

Serving: Serves 8–10 | Prep: | Ready in:

Ingredients

- 1/4 pound leaf lard, cut into large cubes, at room temperature, plus a little to grease the pan
- 1 cup packed light brown sugar
- 3/4 cup plus 2 tablespoons all-purpose flour
- 3/4 cup plus 1 tablespoon stone-ground white cornmeal
- 1 teaspoon baking powder
- 1 teaspoon baking soda
- 1 teaspoon salt
- 1 1/2 tablespoons ground ginger
- 1 1/2 teaspoons ground cinnamon
- 1/2 teaspoon freshly grated nutmeg
- 1/8 teaspoon ground cloves
- 1 cup apple butter
- 1 cup whole buttermilk
- 2 tablespoons bourbon
- 2 large eggs
- 1 large egg yolk
- 1 cup sorghum syrup
- 1/2 cup heavy cream

Direction

- Preheat an oven to 350°F. Oil a round cake pan of 10-inch in size.

- In the bowl of stand mixer fitted with paddle attachment, put the brown sugar and lard. Process on low speed to blend, and then raise the speed to high to cream them together. Process till mixture turns smooth and very light brown, scraping down sides of bowl as necessary for approximately 20 minutes.
- In the meantime, in a big bowl, mix together the cloves, nutmeg, cinnamon, ginger, salt, baking soda, baking powder, cornmeal and flour. Mix together the bourbon, buttermilk and apple butter in another big bowl.
- Lower the speed to moderate when lard-sugar mixture is ready, and put in egg yolk and eggs, one by one, till blended. Put the flour mixture in thirds, alternately with apple butter mixture, whisking barely till batter is smooth each time.
- In the prepped cake pan, put the batter and Bake for 40 to 45 minutes, till a toothpick pricked in the middle comes out dry. Transfer the pan onto a rack to let cool while you prepare the syrup.
- In a heavy-bottomed saucepan, mix cream and sorghum, and boil. Then lower heat to low and allow to simmer for 10 minutes. Mix till well incorporated.
- On a serving plate, put the cake. Using a fork, puncture holes throughout top of cake, and gently pour the syrup over the entire cake till it has been soaked up. Serve lightly warm.

Nutrition Information

- Calories: 625
- Saturated Fat: 11 g(56%)
- Sodium: 498 mg(21%)
- Fiber: 2 g(8%)
- Total Carbohydrate: 99 g(33%)
- Cholesterol: 109 mg(36%)
- Protein: 6 g(13%)
- Total Fat: 22 g(34%)

24. Crystallized Ginger Spice Bars

Serving: Makes about 46 bars | Prep: | Ready in:

Ingredients

- 3 cups all-purpose flour
- 1 teaspoon baking soda
- 1/2 teaspoon salt
- 2 teaspoons ground ginger
- 1/2 teaspoon ground cloves
- 1/4 teaspoon ground cinnamon
- 2 sticks (1 cup) unsalted butter, softened
- 1 cup sugar
- 1/2 cup unsulfured molasses
- 1 large egg
- 3 ounces crystallized ginger, chopped coarse (about 1/2 cup)
- 1 1/2 tablespoons freshly grated orange zest

Direction

- Whisk ground spices, salt, baking soda and flour in a bowl. Use electric mixer to beat sugar and butter till fluffy and light in another bowl. Add zest, crystallized ginger, flour mixture, egg and molasses; beat till dough forms.
- Pat dough to 1-in. thick, 8x5-in. rectangle on wax paper sheet; chill dough till firm or for 4 hours, wrapped in wax paper.
- You can keep dough in the fridge for 1 week or freeze for 1 month after being shaped to rectangle. Thaw frozen dough in fridge for 4 hours till sliceable; you can keep baked cookies for 4 days in airtight containers at room temperature.
- Preheat the oven to 350°F and coat 2 baking sheets with butter lightly.
- Crosswise cut dough to 1/6-in. thick slices; put on baking sheets, 2-in. apart. In batches, bake bars for 8-10 minutes till deep golden brown in center of oven. Put on racks; cool. You can keep baked cookies for 4 days in airtight containers at room temperature.

Nutrition Information

- Calories: 102
- Sodium: 58 mg(2%)
- Fiber: 0 g(1%)
- Total Carbohydrate: 15 g(5%)
- Cholesterol: 15 mg(5%)
- Protein: 1 g(2%)
- Total Fat: 4 g(6%)
- Saturated Fat: 3 g(13%)

25. Cumin Scented Eggplant With Pomegranate And Cilantro

Serving: Makes 4 servings | Prep: | Ready in:

Ingredients

- 5 cups water
- 2 1/2 tablespoons sea salt or coarse kosher salt
- 2 pounds eggplant (about 2 medium), cut crosswise into 1/2-inch-thick slices
- 1 tablespoon (or more) olive oil
- 2 teaspoons ground cumin
- 1/8 teaspoon cayenne pepper
- 2 garlic cloves, minced
- Pomegranate molasses* (for drizzling)
- 2/3 cup pomegranate seeds
- 1/4 cup cilantro leaves

Direction

- Mix 2 1/2 tbsp. of sea salt and 5 cups of water in a large bowl until the salt is dissolved. Add the eggplant slices. Place plate on the eggplant to submerge. Let it soak for 1 hour. Drain the eggplant and pat it to dry.
- Set the oven to 350°F for preheating. Put 1 tbsp. of olive oil in a large nonstick skillet and heat it over medium-high heat. Working in batches, cook each side of the eggplant for 2 minutes until its spots are browned and softened. Arrange the cooked eggplant on a large rimmed baking sheet. Do the same with the remaining eggplant. If necessary, add more tablespoonfuls of oil into the skillet. Arrange the eggplant in a single layer on the baking sheet.
- Combine cayenne and cumin and sprinkle the mixture into the eggplant. Roast for 30 minutes until cooked through and golden.
- Remove the eggplant from the oven and sprinkle it with garlic. On a platter, arrange the eggplant and drizzle it with pomegranate molasses lightly. Sprinkle it with cilantro and pomegranate seeds. Best when served warm or at room temperature.
- Note: The thick pomegranate syrup is available at some supermarkets, online, and some Middle Eastern markets.

Nutrition Information

- Calories: 117
- Saturated Fat: 1 g(4%)
- Sodium: 1309 mg(55%)
- Fiber: 8 g(33%)
- Total Carbohydrate: 20 g(7%)
- Protein: 3 g(6%)
- Total Fat: 4 g(7%)

26. Currant And Molasses Spice Cookies

Serving: Makes about 64 cookies | Prep: | Ready in:

Ingredients

- 1 1/2 sticks (3/4 cup) unsalted butter, softened
- 1/2 cup sugar
- 1/3 cup unsulfured molasses
- 2 cups all-purpose flour
- 1/2 teaspoon baking soda
- 1/2 teaspoon salt
- 1 1/2 teaspoon ground ginger
- 3/4 teaspoon cinnamon
- 1/4 teaspoon ground cloves
- 1/2 cup dried currants, soaked in boiling water to cover for 5 minutes, drained, and patted dry

Direction

- Cream the sugar and butter in a bowl using an electric mixer till mixture is fluffy and light and mix in molasses. Sift together the spices, salt, baking soda and flour into the bowl, beat dough till incorporated thoroughly, and mix in currants. Divide the dough in half and shape every half on a sheet of wax paper forming an 8-inch log, with wax paper to support. Refrigerate the logs, covered in wax paper for a minimum of 4 hours or overnight.
- Preheat an oven to 350°F. Using a sharp knife, slice the logs into quarter-inch thick portions and on slightly buttered baking sheets, set the portions 2-inch away. Working in batches, let the cookies bake in the center of oven for 10 to 12 minutes, or till pale golden. To racks, put the cookies and allow to cool.

Nutrition Information

- Calories: 48
- Fiber: 0 g(1%)
- Total Carbohydrate: 7 g(2%)
- Cholesterol: 6 mg(2%)
- Protein: 0 g(1%)
- Total Fat: 2 g(3%)
- Saturated Fat: 1 g(7%)
- Sodium: 26 mg(1%)

27. Dark Ginger Rye Cake With Yogurt And Honey

Serving: Makes one 10-inch cake | Prep: | Ready in:

Ingredients

- Nonstick vegetable oil spray
- 1 cup robust-flavored (dark) molasses (not blackstrap)
- 1 cup stout
- 1/2 teaspoon baking soda
- 1 1/2 cups rye flour
- 1/2 cup all-purpose flour
- 2 tablespoons ground ginger
- 1 teaspoon ground cinnamon
- 1/4 teaspoon freshly grated nutmeg
- 1/2 teaspoon freshly ground black pepper
- 1 1/2 teaspoons baking powder
- 1 teaspoon kosher salt
- 3 large eggs
- 1 cup granulated sugar
- 1 cup (packed) dark brown sugar
- 1 teaspoon finely grated peeled ginger
- 1 teaspoon vanilla extract
- 1/2 cup virgin coconut oil, melted, slightly cooled
- 1/4 cup vegetable oil
- 1/4 cup honey
- 2 cups plain whole-milk yogurt
- A 10-inch-diameter springform pan

Direction

- Preheat an oven to 350°F. With nonstick spray, slightly grease the pan. In a small saucepan, simmer stout and molasses, mixing to blend. Take off heat and mix in the baking soda; allow to cool.
- Through a coarse-mesh sieve set over a medium bowl, sift pepper, nutmeg, cinnamon, ground ginger, all-purpose flour and rye flour. Mix in the salt and baking powder. In a big bowl, mix vanilla extract, fresh ginger, brown sugar, granulated sugar and eggs to incorporate. Mix in the cooled molasses mixture, vegetable oil and coconut oil. Put to dry ingredients and fold till incorporated. Into prepped pan, scrape the batter.
- Allow the cake to bake for 1 hour till a tester pricked into the middle comes out clean. To a wire rack, put the pan and allow the cake to cool for 10 minutes in pan. Trace a knife around the sides of cake and release from mold. Let cool fully.
- Cut the cake into big portions and set on a platter. In a small bowl, twirl honey into the yogurt and serve along with cake.
- Cake can be prepared 3 days in advance. Keep securely wrapped at room temperature.

Nutrition Information

- Calories: 5977
- Saturated Fat: 116 g(578%)
- Sodium: 3703 mg(154%)
- Fiber: 23 g(93%)
- Total Carbohydrate: 946 g(315%)
- Cholesterol: 622 mg(207%)
- Protein: 62 g(124%)
- Total Fat: 228 g(351%)

28. Giant Pumpkin Muffins With Molasses Ginger Glaze

Serving: Makes 6 giant muffins or 18 standard muffins | Prep: | Ready in:

Ingredients

- Nonstick vegetable oil spray
- 2 3/4 cups all purpose flour
- 2 teaspoons ground ginger
- 1 1/2 teaspoons baking soda
- 1 teaspoon salt
- 1 cup sugar
- 1/2 cup canola oil
- 3 large eggs
- 1 15-ounce can pure pumpkin
- 1/2 cup plus 1 tablespoon mild-flavored (light) molasses
- 1/2 cup buttermilk
- 1/2 cup chopped crystallized ginger, divided
- 1 1/2 cups powdered sugar
- 1 1/2 tablespoons (or more) water

Direction

- Preheat an oven to 350°F. With nonstick spray, coat 18 standard 1/3-cup muffin cups or 6 huge 1 1/4-cup muffin cups. In medium bowl, sift salt, baking soda, ginger and flour. In big bowl, whisk oil and a cup of sugar with electric mixer to incorporate. Whisk in eggs, one by one, mixing thoroughly after each addition. Whisk in 1/4 cup crystallized ginger, buttermilk, 1/2 cup molasses and pumpkin. Mix in the flour mixture till just incorporated.
- Distribute the batter into prepped muffin cups. Bake till toothpick pricked into middle comes out clean, 40 minutes for giant muffins and half an hour for standard muffins. Move the muffins to rack; cool fully.
- In medium bowl, beat 1 tablespoon molasses, 1 1/2 tablespoons water and powdered sugar, putting additional water as necessary to create a thick glaze.
- In glaze, dunk the muffin tops; move to rack, letting glaze to drip down the sides. Scatter 1/4 cup crystallized ginger on top. Allow to sit for 1 hour till glaze is set.

Nutrition Information

- Calories: 874
- Cholesterol: 94 mg(31%)
- Protein: 11 g(21%)
- Total Fat: 26 g(40%)
- Saturated Fat: 3 g(14%)
- Sodium: 732 mg(31%)
- Fiber: 4 g(16%)
- Total Carbohydrate: 153 g(51%)

29. Ginger Date Muffins

Serving: Makes 12 muffins | Prep: | Ready in:

Ingredients

- 1 1/4 cups all-purpose flour
- 1 teaspoon ground ginger
- 1/2 teaspoon baking powder
- 1/4 teaspoon baking soda
- 1/4 teaspoon salt
- 1 large egg
- 6 tablespoons unsulfured molasses
- 1 3/4 cups packed pitted dates (about 10 ounces)

- 1 1/2 sticks (3/4 cup) unsalted butter, softened
- 6 tablespoons packed dark brown sugar

Direction

- Preheat an oven to 400°F. Butter a dozen 1/3-cup muffin cups.
- Sift salt, baking soda, baking powder, ginger and flour in a bowl. Whisk molasses and egg till combined in a small bowl. Chop dates coarsely. Use electric mixer to beat sugar and butter till fluffy and light in a big bowl; beat in egg mixtures and flour till just combined. Mix in dates; divide batter between muffin cups. Bake for 15 minutes in center of oven till tester exits clean; muffins won't dome.

Nutrition Information

- Calories: 276
- Protein: 2 g(5%)
- Total Fat: 12 g(19%)
- Saturated Fat: 7 g(37%)
- Sodium: 103 mg(4%)
- Fiber: 2 g(8%)
- Total Carbohydrate: 42 g(14%)
- Cholesterol: 46 mg(15%)

30. Ginger Molasses Lace Cookies

Serving: Makes about 60 cookies | Prep: | Ready in:

Ingredients

- 1/2 cup packed light brown sugar
- 3/4 stick (6 tablespoons) unsalted butter
- 2 tablespoons unsulfured molasses
- 1 tablespoon fresh lemon juice
- 1/3 cup all-purpose flour
- 1 teaspoon ground ginger

Direction

- Over medium heat, boil lemon juice, molasses, butter and sugar in a 1- to 1 1/2-quart heavy saucepan, mixing, and boil for a minute. Take pan off heat and mix in a pinch salt, ginger and flour till mixture is smooth. Let the dough cool to room temperature. Shape and bake the cookies as instructed below.
- To shape and bake the lace cookies: preheat an oven to 350°F and with parchment paper, line 2 big baking sheets.
- Roll out level half-teaspoon dough into rounds and on baking sheets, set 4-inch away. In upper and lower thirds of oven, let the cookies bake for 10 minutes in batches, changing place of sheets midway through baking, or till cookies are golden and flat. To racks, put the parchment with cookies to cool. Allow the baking sheets to cool and line with new parchment among batches.

Nutrition Information

- Calories: 22
- Cholesterol: 3 mg(1%)
- Protein: 0 g(0%)
- Total Fat: 1 g(2%)
- Saturated Fat: 1 g(4%)
- Sodium: 1 mg(0%)
- Fiber: 0 g(0%)
- Total Carbohydrate: 3 g(1%)

31. Ginger Molasses Cake

Serving: Makes 12 servings | Prep: | Ready in:

Ingredients

- 3 1/4 cups all purpose flour
- 5 teaspoons ground ginger
- 2 1/2 teaspoons baking soda
- 1 1/2 teaspoons ground cinnamon
- 1/4 teaspoon salt
- 1 cup mild-flavored (light) molasses
- 1 cup sugar
- 1/4 cup sour cream
- 2 large eggs

- 2 teaspoons vanilla extract
- 1 cup boiling water
- 1 cup vegetable oil
- Purchased caramel sauce, warmed
- Whipped cream

Direction

- Preheat an oven to 350°F. Butter and flour 12-cup Bundt pan. Into medium bowl, sift the initial 5 ingredients. In a big bowl, mix vanilla, eggs, sour cream, sugar and molasses till well incorporated. Mix in oil and a cup of boiling water, then the dry ingredients. Put the batter into prepped pan.
- Let the cake bake for 45 minutes till tester pricked into middle comes out clean. Allow to cool for 20 minutes in pan on rack. Transfer onto a plate; cool fully. Can be done a day in advance. Put a cover and keep at room temperature. Slice the cake into wedges. Serve along with whipped cream and warm caramel sauce.

Nutrition Information

32. Ginger Spice Cookies

Serving: Makes about 28 | Prep: | Ready in:

Ingredients

- 1 1/4 cups all purpose flour
- 1 teaspoon ground cinnamon
- 1 teaspoon ground ginger
- 1/2 teaspoon baking soda
- 1/4 teaspoon salt
- 1/4 teaspoon ground cloves
- 1/2 cup (1 stick) unsalted butter, room temperature
- 2/3 cup (packed) golden brown sugar
- 1 large egg
- 2 tablespoons mild-flavored (light) molasses
- Sugar

Direction

- In a medium bowl, combine cloves, salt, baking soda, ginger, cinnamon and flour. In a big bowl, whisk the brown sugar and butter till fluffy. Whisk in the molasses and egg. Whisk in the dry ingredients, dough will become really soft. Put plastic to cover the bowl. Chill overnight.
- Preheat an oven to 325°F. Slightly grease 2 big baking sheets with butter. In a shallow dish, put the sugar. Shape the dough into 1 1/4-inch rounds. To coat, roll every round in sugar. Set cookies on prepped baking sheets, setting 2-inch away. Softly press dough rounds to create 1 1/2- to 1 3/4-inch circles with bottom of glass. Allow to bake for 12 minutes till cookies slightly puff yet remain soft. To rack, put the cookies and let cool. Can be made 3 days in advance. Keep in an airtight container.

Nutrition Information

- Calories: 77
- Saturated Fat: 2 g(11%)
- Sodium: 43 mg(2%)
- Fiber: 0 g(1%)
- Total Carbohydrate: 11 g(4%)
- Cholesterol: 15 mg(5%)
- Protein: 1 g(2%)
- Total Fat: 4 g(5%)

33. Gingerbread Bars

Serving: Makes 24 | Prep: | Ready in:

Ingredients

- 2 cups all purpose flour
- 2 teaspoons ground ginger
- 1 teaspoon ground cinnamon
- 1/4 teaspoon ground nutmeg

- 1/4 teaspoon ground cloves
- 1/2 teaspoon baking soda
- 1/2 teaspoon salt
- 10 tablespoons (1 1/4 sticks) unsalted butter, room temperature
- 3/4 cup (packed) dark brown sugar
- 7 1/2 tablespoons sugar, divided
- 2 large eggs
- 1/4 cup light (unsulfured) molasses

Direction

- Preheat an oven to 350°F. Butter and flour a baking sheet, 15x10x1-inch in size. In a medium bowl, put 2 cups of flour; to a small bowl, put the 2 tablespoons flour and set aside. To flour in medium bowl, put salt, baking soda and spices; beat to combine. In a big bowl, mix 6 tablespoons sugar, brown sugar and butter with electric mixer till fluffy. Mix in the eggs, one by one, then the molasses. To butter mixture, put the dry ingredients and mix to incorporate. In prepped pan, scatter the batter evenly. On top of the batter, sift the reserved 2 tablespoons flour equally, then scatter leftover 1 1/2 tablespoons sugar equally.
- Let the gingerbread bake for 22 minutes till golden brown and tester pricked into middle comes out clean; cool fully in pan on the rack. Slice gingerbread crosswise making 4 strips, then slice every strip into 6 portions, creating 2 dozen bars, each approximately 3 1/2 x 1 3/4 inches. Can be prepared 2 days in advance. Keep airtight at room temperature.

Nutrition Information

- Calories: 139
- Protein: 2 g(3%)
- Total Fat: 5 g(8%)
- Saturated Fat: 3 g(16%)
- Sodium: 82 mg(3%)
- Fiber: 0 g(1%)
- Total Carbohydrate: 22 g(7%)
- Cholesterol: 28 mg(9%)

34. Gingerbread Cake

Serving: Makes 8 servings | Prep: 15mins | Ready in:

Ingredients

- Nonstick vegetable oil spray
- 1 1/2 cups all-purpose flour
- 1 teaspoon ground ginger
- 3/4 teaspoon ground cinnamon
- 3/4 teaspoon kosher salt
- 1/2 teaspoon baking powder
- 1/2 teaspoon baking soda
- 1/2 cup (1 stick) unsalted butter, cut into 1/2" pieces
- 1/2 cup (packed) light brown sugar
- 1/2 cup mild-flavored (light) molasses
- 1 large egg, beaten to blend
- 2 teaspoons grated peeled ginger
- 1 cup chilled heavy cream
- 1 tablespoon powdered sugar
- 1/4 cup store-bought lemon curd
- Finely grated lemon zest
- An 8" square metal cake pan

Direction

- Cake: Preheat an oven to 350°F. Use nonstick spray to coat pan; line parchment paper on bottom. Spray paper. Whisk flour then following 5 ingredients in a medium bowl; put butter in a big bowl. Put 1/2 cup boiling water over; whisk till melted. Whisk in sugar then the following 3 ingredients. Add dry ingredients then whisk to blend; put in prepped pan.
- Bake for 25 minutes till inserted tester in middle of cake exits clean; cool for 10 minutes in pan. Invert on a wire rack; cool. Remove parchment.
- Topping: beat sugar and cream till firm peaks form in a medium bowl; fold in curd, leaving swirls then spread on cake. Use zest to garnish.

35. Gingerbread Candy Canes

Serving: Makes 5 to 6 dozen cookies (depending on size of cookie cutter) | Prep: | Ready in:

Ingredients

- 2 sticks (1/2 pound) unsalted butter, softened
- 1 cup sugar
- 1 tablespoon ground ginger
- 1 tablespoon ground cinnamon
- 2 teaspoons ground allspice
- 1 teaspoon baking soda
- 1/2 teaspoon ground cloves
- 1 large egg
- 4 cups all-purpose flour
- 1 cup unsulfured molasses
- Red and green sanding sugar, for decorating

Direction

- At high speed, beat sugar and butter in electric mixer for 5 minutes till fluffy. Put cloves, baking soda, allspice, cinnamon and ginger and blend at low speed till incorporated. Mix in the egg. Put in 2 cups of flour and blend at low speed till just blended. Mix in the molasses till just incorporated. Put in leftover 2 cups flour and blend at low speed till just mixed. Split dough into 3 parts, shape into 3 disks, and wrap with waxed paper or plastic wrap. Refrigerate till firm for a minimum of 1 hour up to 2 days.
- In upper and lower thirds of the oven, set the racks and preheat the oven to 375°F. With parchment paper, line 2 heavy big baking sheets.
- Take 1 dough disk out of refrigerator. Unroll dough to 1/4- to 1/8-inch thickness on slightly floured work surface. Cut out cookies with 3- to 4-inch candy cane cookie cutter; using a spatula, move to baking sheets. Gather together and roll again the scraps and cut out more cookies. Jazz up with green and red sanding sugar stripes, then refrigerate cookies for 10 minutes.
- Bake for 10 minutes till aromatic and lightly colored. Allow to cool on pans for 2 minutes, then turn onto racks and cool fully. Redo with the rest of the dough.

Nutrition Information

- Calories: 81
- Total Carbohydrate: 13 g(4%)
- Cholesterol: 10 mg(3%)
- Protein: 1 g(2%)
- Total Fat: 3 g(5%)
- Saturated Fat: 2 g(9%)
- Sodium: 23 mg(1%)
- Fiber: 0 g(1%)

36. Gingerbread Layer Cake With Cream Cheese Frosting And Candied Pistachios

Serving: Makes 10 servings | Prep: | Ready in:

Ingredients

- 1 cup Guinness extra stout or dark beer
- 1 cup mild-flavored (light) molasses
- 1 1/2 teaspoons baking soda
- 2 cups all purpose flour
- 2 tablespoons ground ginger
- 1 1/2 teaspoons baking powder
- 3/4 teaspoon ground cinnamon
- 1/4 teaspoon ground cloves
- 1/4 teaspoon ground nutmeg
- 1/8 teaspoon ground cardamom
- 3 large eggs
- 1/2 cup sugar
- 1/2 cup (packed) dark brown sugar
- 3/4 cup vegetable oil
- 1 tablespoon minced peeled fresh ginger

- 1 cup finely chopped pistachios
- 1 tablespoon light corn syrup
- 2 tablespoons sugar
- 2 8-ounce packages cream cheese, room temperature
- 1/2 cup (1 stick) unsalted butter, room temperature
- 3/4 teaspoon finely grated orange peel
- 2 cups powdered sugar

Direction

- For cake: preheat an oven to 350°F. Butter and flour 3 cake pans of 8-inch diameter. In heavy medium saucepan, boil molasses and stout over high heat. Take away from heat; mix in the baking soda. Allow to sit for 1 hour to cool fully.
- In big bowl, mix the flour and following 6 ingredients to incorporate. In medium bowl, mix both sugars and eggs to incorporate. Mix in the oil, then the stout mixture. Slowly mix the stout-egg mixture into the flour mixture. Mix in the fresh ginger.
- Distribute the batter into prepped pans. Bake for 25 minutes till tester pricked into centers of cakes comes out clean. Cool the cakes in pans for 15 minutes. Flip cakes over onto racks; let cool. Cake can be made a day in advance. Wrap each cake in plastic individually and store at room temperature.
- For the candied pistachios: preheat an oven to 325°F. With foil, line big baking sheet. In medium bowl, combine corn syrup and pistachios. Put in the sugar and coat by tossing. Working briskly so sugar won't melt, on prepped baking sheet, spread pistachios. Bake for 8 minutes till pistachios are light golden. Cool fully. Pistachios can be prepared a day in advance. Keep airtight at room temperature.
- For the cream cheese frosting: in big bowl, beat orange peel, butter and cream cheese with an electric mixer till fluffy. Slowly mix in the powdered sugar. Refrigerate frosting for 30 minutes.
- On a platter, put a cake layer, rounded side facing up. Spread 3/4 cup of frosting on top. Put another layer of cake on top, rounded side facing up, then spread 3/4 cup of the frosting on top. Put the third layer of cake on top, flat side facing up. Spread sides and top of the cake with the rest of frosting. Spread candied pistachios on top of the cake. The cake can be prepared a day in advance. Put on a cover and chill. Bring to room temperature prior to serving. Slice cake into wedges, serve.

Nutrition Information

- Calories: 870
- Total Fat: 49 g(75%)
- Saturated Fat: 17 g(85%)
- Sodium: 451 mg(19%)
- Fiber: 2 g(9%)
- Total Carbohydrate: 101 g(34%)
- Cholesterol: 130 mg(43%)
- Protein: 10 g(20%)

37. Gingerbread With Crystallized Ginger

Serving: Serves 16 | Prep: | Ready in:

Ingredients

- 1 1/2 cups all purpose flour
- 1 teaspoon ground cinnamon
- 3/4 teaspoon ground ginger
- 1/2 teaspoon baking powder
- 1/2 teaspoon baking soda
- 1/2 teaspoon salt
- 1/4 teaspoon ground nutmeg
- 1/2 cup (1 stick) unsalted butter, room temperature
- 1/2 cup (packed) dark brown sugar
- 1/2 cup robust (dark) molasses
- 1 large egg
- 1/2 cup pear nectar
- 1/4 cup chopped crystallized ginger

- Powdered sugar

Direction

- Preheat the oven to 350°F. Butter and flour a baking pan, 8x8x2-inch in size. In a medium bowl, combine the initial 7 ingredients. In a big bowl, whisk brown sugar and butter till fluffy. Put the egg and molasses and whisk to incorporate. Whisk in the pear nectar, then the chopped ginger and dry ingredients. Put the batter to pan.
- Let the cake bake for 35 minutes till tester pricked into middle comes out clean. Put the pan to rack; allow the cake to cool for 15 minutes. Sift the powdered sugar on top of cake. Slice the cake into 16 cubes. Serve at room temperature or while warm.

Nutrition Information

- Calories: 174
- Cholesterol: 27 mg(9%)
- Protein: 2 g(3%)
- Total Fat: 6 g(10%)
- Saturated Fat: 4 g(19%)
- Sodium: 121 mg(5%)
- Fiber: 1 g(2%)
- Total Carbohydrate: 29 g(10%)

38. Gingerbread With Vanilla Ice Cream And Exotic Caramel Sauce

Serving: Makes 8 servings | Prep: | Ready in:

Ingredients

- 2 1/2 cups plus 2 teaspoons all purpose flour
- 2 1/2 teaspoons ground ginger
- 1 teaspoon ground cinnamon
- 1 teaspoon salt
- 3/4 cup chopped crystallized ginger (about 5 ounces)
- 1/2 cup (1 stick) unsalted butter, room temperature
- 1/2 cup (packed) golden brown sugar
- 1 cup mild-flavored (light) molasses
- 1 cup boiling water
- 2 teaspoons baking soda
- 1 large egg, beaten to blend
- Vanilla ice cream
- Exotic Caramel Sauce

Direction

- Preheat the oven to 375°F. Slightly butter a baking pan, 13x9x2-inch in size. Into medium bowl, sift salt, cinnamon, ground ginger and 2 1/2 cups flour. In a small bowl, combine 2 teaspoons flour and crystallized ginger.
- In a big bowl, whisk butter with an electric mixer till fluffy. Put the brown sugar and whisk till mixture is fluffy and light. In a separate medium bowl, combine baking soda, 1 cup boiling water and molasses to incorporate. Mix into the butter mixture. Mix in the dry ingredients, then the crystallized ginger mixture and egg. Into the prepped pan, put the batter.
- Allow the cake to bake for 15 minutes. Lower the oven temperature to 350°F and let the cake bake for 12 minutes more till tester pricked into middle comes out clean. Put the pan to a rack; let cool for half an hour. Transfer the cake onto rack; allow to cool. Can be prepared 8 hours in advance. Place a cover; keep at room temperature.
- Slice gingerbread into portions. Put the gingerbread to plates. Place ice cream on top of each portion. Scoop Exotic Caramel Sauce on top and serve.

Nutrition Information

39. Gingersnaps

Serving: Makes about 56 cookies | Prep: | Ready in:

Ingredients

- 2 1/4 cups all-purpose flour
- 1 teaspoon baking soda
- 1 1/2 teaspoons ground ginger
- 1 teaspoon ground cinnamon
- 1/2 teaspoon ground cloves
- 1 cup packed brown sugar
- 1 1/2 sticks (3/4 cup) unsalted butter
- 1/4 cup unsulfured molasses
- 1 large egg
- parchment paper
- 1/4 cup granulated sugar

Direction

- Sift together spices, baking soda and 1 cup plus 2 tablespoons flour into a big bowl and mix in the brown sugar. Liquify the butter in a small saucepan and mix into the flour mixture together with egg and molasses till well blended. Mix in leftover 1 cup plus 2 tablespoons flour with a wooden spoon till blended thoroughly. Refrigerate the dough with a cover, till firm, for a minimum of an hour up to 2 days.
- Preheat the oven to 350°F and line parchment paper on baking sheets.
- Roll level tablespoons of dough into rounds and to coat, roll rounds in granulated sugar in a small bowl. On baking sheets, place the rounds approximately 2 inches away and in batches, let bake in center of the oven for 10 to 12 minutes till a shade darker and flattened. Cookies will slightly puff then subside slightly, and surface will be covered with small cracks. Allow the cookies to cool on baking sheets for 2 minutes and using a spatula, put to racks to cool fully. Cookies keep at room temperature in an airtight container for 5 days.

Nutrition Information

- Calories: 64
- Fiber: 0 g(1%)
- Total Carbohydrate: 10 g(3%)
- Cholesterol: 10 mg(3%)
- Protein: 1 g(1%)
- Total Fat: 3 g(4%)
- Saturated Fat: 2 g(8%)
- Sodium: 26 mg(1%)

40. Grilled Corn On The Cob With Chipotle, Molasses, And Orange Glaze

Serving: Makes 6 servings | Prep: | Ready in:

Ingredients

- 1/4 cup (1/2 stick) unsalted butter
- 2 tablespoons frozen orange juice concentrate
- 2 teaspoons minced canned chipotle chiles
- 2 teaspoons mild-flavored (light) molasses
- 1/4 teaspoon salt
- 2 tablespoons chopped fresh cilantro
- 6 ears of corn, shucked

Direction

- Set grill on medium-high heat. Combine in a microwave-safe bowl the butter, chipotle chilies, concentrated orange juice, salt and molasses. Melt it on high in microwave for at least 20 seconds (or on medium-low heat, get a saucepan and melt butter before adding next 4 ingredients). Add in cilantro. Barbeque corn occasionally flipping it for at least 3 minutes until black spots appear. Coat generously with glaze. Barbeque it again for at least 3 minutes until glaze sets. Put on a platter and coat the corn with more glaze. Pass the leftover glaze and salt separately while serving.

Nutrition Information

- Calories: 206

- Sodium: 124 mg(5%)
- Fiber: 4 g(14%)
- Total Carbohydrate: 33 g(11%)
- Cholesterol: 20 mg(7%)
- Protein: 4 g(9%)
- Total Fat: 9 g(13%)
- Saturated Fat: 5 g(25%)

41. Grilled Molasses And Rum Glazed Fresh Ham

Serving: Makes 10 to 12 servings | Prep: 30mins | Ready in:

Ingredients

- 4 quarts water
- 1 cup sugar
- 1 cup table salt
- 30 whole cloves
- 4 whole nutmegs, cracked
- 1 (8- to 10-lb) bone-in shank-end fresh ham, skinned and trimmed of all but a thin layer of fat
- 2 tablespoons plus 2 teaspoons coriander seeds
- 4 teaspoons cumin seeds
- 4 teaspoons whole black peppercorns
- 4 teaspoons paprika
- 4 teaspoons kosher salt
- 1/4 cup dark rum
- 1/4 cup molasses (preferably mildly flavored)
- 1/2 stick (1/4 cup) unsalted butter

Direction

- Brine ham: Boil all brining ingredients except for ham in a deep 8-9-qt. pot like pasta pot till salt and sugar dissolves, occasionally mixing. Take off heat; add ham. Make more brine if needed; brine should cover ham. Cool mixture for 30 minutes; chill for a minimum of 1 day and up to 2 days, covered, flipping ham 1 or 2 times.
- Use enough hardwood charcoal to prep grill for cooking to fill shoe box or charcoal chimney. Push coals to 1 side of grill when they're ready; leave 2/3 of grill free from coals. Opposite coals, put a drip pan.
- Cook ham and make spice rub; grind all spice-rub ingredients in a spice or electric coffee grinder finely.
- Drain ham; pat dry. Massage ground spices all over ham.
- Put ham, fatty side up, on grill rack over drip pan. Cover the grill; leave bottom vents fully open and cover vents 1/4 open; cook ham, putting big handful of charcoal every 30 minutes. Flip ham after 1 hour so opposite side faces coals; cook for 1-2 more hours till an inserted meat thermometer near yet not touching bone reads 155°F.
- As ham grills, make glaze: Heat glaze ingredients on medium heat till butter melts, mixing.
- Brush glaze on ham a few times at final 30 minutes of grilling; let excess fall into the drip pan.
- Serve ham: put cooked ham on a platter; loosely cover with foil. Stand ham before carving for 30-60 minutes. Serve alongside pan drippings or skimmed off fat.

Nutrition Information

- Calories: 1004
- Saturated Fat: 25 g(127%)
- Sodium: 1935 mg(81%)
- Fiber: 2 g(6%)
- Total Carbohydrate: 29 g(10%)
- Cholesterol: 260 mg(87%)
- Protein: 60 g(119%)
- Total Fat: 69 g(107%)

42. Grilled Pork Tenderloin With Molasses And Mustard

Serving: Makes 2 servings | Prep: 30mins | Ready in:

Ingredients

- 1/4 cup mild-flavored (light) molasses
- 3 tablespoons apple cider vinegar, divided
- 2 tablespoons Dijon mustard
- 2 tablespoons coarse-grained mustard
- 1 3/4-pound pork tenderloin

Direction

- In small bowl, mix both mustards, 2 tablespoons vinegar and molasses to incorporate. Put the pork in heavy-duty plastic bag that is resealable. Pour in the marinade. Enclose tightly and chill for 4 hours.
- Prepare barbecue ready at moderately-high heat. Drain the marinade into a heavy small saucepan. Scatter pepper and salt on pork. Grill the pork for 20 minutes till thermometer pricked into middle reads 145°F, flipping from time to time using tongs. Move the pork to serving platter; allow to sit for 5 minutes.
- In the meantime, in the pan with marinade, put 1 tablespoon of vinegar and boil for 1 minute till thickened to sauce consistency.
- Slice the pork crosswise on slight diagonal into half-inch-thick portions. Set the pork slices on the platter; sprinkle sauce on top.

Nutrition Information

- Calories: 621
- Saturated Fat: 5 g(24%)
- Sodium: 554 mg(23%)
- Fiber: 1 g(5%)
- Total Carbohydrate: 33 g(11%)
- Cholesterol: 258 mg(86%)
- Protein: 83 g(166%)
- Total Fat: 15 g(23%)

43. Guinness Stout Ginger Cake

Serving: Makes 8 servings | Prep: | Ready in:

Ingredients

- 1 cup Guinness stout
- 1 cup molasses
- 1/2 tablespoon baking soda
- 3 large eggs
- 1/2 cup granulated sugar
- 1/2 cup firmly packed dark brown sugar
- 3/4 cup grapeseed or vegetable oil
- 2 cups all-purpose flour
- 2 tablespoons ground ginger
- 1 1/2 teaspoons baking powder
- 3/4 teaspoon ground cinnamon
- 1/4 teaspoon ground cloves
- 1/4 teaspoon freshly grated nutmeg
- 1/8 teaspoon ground cardamom
- 1 tablespoon grated, peeled fresh gingerroot

Direction

- Preheat an oven to 350°F then butter 9x5-in. loaf pan; line parchment on sides and bottom. Grease parchment. Otherwise, butter then flour a 6-cup Bundt pan.
- Boil molasses and stout in a big saucepan on high heat; turn heat off. Add baking soda; allow to stand till foam dissipates.
- Meanwhile, whisk both sugars and eggs in a bowl; whisk in oil.
- Whisk cardamom, nutmeg, cloves, cinnamon, baking powder, ground ginger and flour in another bowl.
- Mix stout mixture with egg mixture; whisk this liquid, 1/2 at a time, into flour mixture. Add fresh ginger; mix to combine.
- Put batter in the loaf pan; bake till gently pressing top makes it spring back or for 1 hour. Don't open the oven till gingerbread is nearly done or center could slightly fall. Put on wire rack; cool.

Nutrition Information

- Calories: 568
- Total Carbohydrate: 84 g(28%)
- Cholesterol: 70 mg(23%)
- Protein: 6 g(12%)

- Total Fat: 23 g(36%)
- Saturated Fat: 2 g(10%)
- Sodium: 353 mg(15%)
- Fiber: 1 g(5%)

44. Hot Molasses Milk Punch

Serving: Makes 2 drinks. | Prep: | Ready in:

Ingredients

- 1 tablespoon sugar
- 1 tablespoon unsulfured dark molasses
- 1/4 teaspoon ground ginger
- 2 cups milk
- 1/2 cup dark rum
- freshly grated nutmeg for garnsih

Direction

- Combine ginger, molasses, 1 tbsp. of water and sugar in a saucepan and bring to a simmer while stirring. In a stream, add the milk and whisk. Heat over moderate heat and stir till hot. Don't boil. Add in the rum and stir. Pour the mixture into 2 heated mugs; drizzle some of the nutmeg into each drink.

Nutrition Information

45. Indian Corn Bread Pudding

Serving: Makes 1 serving | Prep: 10mins | Ready in:

Ingredients

- 1 medium corn muffin or 2 corn toaster cakes, cut into 1/2-inch cubes (1 1/4 cups)
- 2/3 cup whole milk
- 1 large egg
- 1 tablespoon molasses
- 1/4 teaspoon ground ginger
- Accompaniment: butter pecan or maple walnut ice cream
- a 12- to 16-oz ceramic baking dish or ovenproof ceramic bowl

Direction

- Preparation Preheat oven to 275°F.
- Put corn bread cubes in baking dish. Whisk together milk, egg, molasses, ginger, and a pinch of salt and pour over bread. Let stand 5 minutes.
- Bake on a baking sheet in middle of oven until edge of custard is just set and center is still wobbly, 40 to 45 minutes. Cool pudding to warm (it will continue to set as it cools).

Nutrition Information

46. Indian Pudding

Serving: 5 | Prep: 20mins | Ready in:

Ingredients

- 4 1/2 cups milk
- 2/3 cup cornmeal
- 1/4 cup butter
- 1/2 cup dark molasses
- 1 teaspoon salt
- 1/4 cup white sugar
- 1 teaspoon ground cinnamon

Direction

- Preheat the oven to 165°C or 325°F. Oil a baking dish, 1 1/2-quart in size.
- In top of double boiler, scald 3 1/2 cups milk over direct heat. Take milk off heat.
- Combine cornmeal with leftover 1 cup milk, and into the scalding milk, mix this mixture, mixing continuously. Into the top of double

boiler, put the milk mixture and allow to cook for 20 minutes, mixing often.
- Into the mixture, mix cinnamon, sugar, salt, molasses and butter. Put into prepped baking dish.
- In the prepped 165°C or 325°F oven, bake for 1 1/2 hours.

Nutrition Information

- Calories: 386 calories;
- Total Fat: 14.2
- Sodium: 638
- Total Carbohydrate: 57.9
- Cholesterol: 42
- Protein: 8.7

47. Indian Pudding With Nutmeg Ice Cream

Serving: Serves 10 | Prep: | Ready in:

Ingredients

- 1 quart vanilla ice cream or frozen vanilla yogurt, slightly softened
- 1 1/2 teaspoons ground nutmeg
- 1/4 cup yellow cornmeal
- 1/4 teaspoon salt
- 3 cups whole milk
- 2 tablespoons (1/4 stick) unsalted butter
- 2 large eggs
- 1/2 cup mild-flavored (light) molasses
- 2 tablespoons (packed) golden brown sugar
- 2 tablespoons sugar
- 1 teaspoon ground ginger
- 1/2 teaspoon ground cinnamon
- 1/3 cup dark or golden raisins

Direction

- Ice cream: in a medium bowl, mix nutmeg and ice cream to incorporate. Cover using foil and put in freezer. Can be made 3 days in advance. Maintain frozen.
- Pudding: preheat an oven to 300°F. Butter a glass baking dish, 8x8x2-inch in size. In a heavy medium saucepan, mix the salt and cornmeal. Slowly mix in 2 1/2 cups of milk. Mix over moderate heat till mixture boils. Lower heat to moderately-low and allow to simmer for 10 minutes till mixture is creamy and thick, mixing frequently. Mix in the butter. Take off heat.
- In a big bowl, mix cinnamon, ground ginger, sugar, brown sugar, molasses and eggs. Slowly mix in the hot cornmeal mixture. Mix in the raisins. Into the prepped baking dish, put the pudding. Add leftover 1/2 cup milk on top of pudding, avoid mixing into pudding. In a big roasting pan, put the pudding dish. Into roasting pan, put sufficient hot water to reach midway up the sides of the pudding dish.
- Let the pudding bake for 1 hour 30 minutes till just set. Take pudding off roasting pan. Let cool for 20 minutes till lukewarm. Can be done 8 hours in advance. Allow to cool; cover using plastic and allow to sit at room temperature. In microwave oven, reheat pudding with a cover on low for 8 minutes.
- Into shallow bowls, scoop warm pudding. Put scoop of ice cream on top.

Nutrition Information

- Calories: 289
- Sodium: 154 mg(6%)
- Fiber: 1 g(4%)
- Total Carbohydrate: 41 g(14%)
- Cholesterol: 74 mg(25%)
- Protein: 6 g(12%)
- Total Fat: 12 g(18%)
- Saturated Fat: 7 g(34%)

48. Individual Ginger Cakes With Apricot Sticky Sauce

Serving: Makes 9 | Prep: | Ready in:

Ingredients

- 2/3 cup dried apricots, thinly sliced
- 3 tablespoons chopped crystallized ginger
- 1 cup sugar
- 3 tablespoons water
- 1 tablespoon light corn syrup
- 1 tablespoon salted butter
- 2/3 cup whipping cream
- 1 teaspoon vanilla extract
- Nonstick vegetable oil spray
- 2 1/2 cups all purpose flour
- 4 teaspoons ground ginger
- 2 teaspoons baking soda
- 1 1/2 teaspoons ground allspice
- 1 cup hot water
- 1 tablespoon instant espresso powder
- 1 cup (packed) golden brown sugar
- 3/4 cup (1 1/2 sticks) salted butter, room temperature
- 1 cup mild-flavored (light) molasses
- 2 large eggs
- 2 tablespoons finely grated peeled fresh ginger
- 2 teaspoons sugar

Direction

- To make sauce: in a small bowl, mix ginger and apricots. Add sufficient boiling water over just to submerge; allow to soften for 10 minutes. Let drain; using paper towels, pat dry.
- In a heavy medium skillet, mix corn syrup, 3 tablespoons water and sugar. Mix over low heat till sugar dissolves. Raise the heat; let boil till syrup turns deep amber color, brushing down the sides using a damp pastry brush and swirling pan from time to time for 10 minutes. Take off from heat. Add in ginger, apricots and butter. Put the vanilla and cream. Mix over low heat till sauce is smooth and caramel bits has dissolved. Can be prepared a day in advance. Put a cover; refrigerate. Over low heat, reheat prior to serving.
- For cakes: preheat the oven to 350°F. With nonstick spray, coat 9 mini-Bundt molds; liberally grease same molds with butter. Into a medium bowl, sift allspice, baking soda, ground ginger and flour. In a small bowl, mix espresso powder and 1 cup hot water and mix to dissolve. In a big bowl, beat butter and brown sugar with an electric mixer till incorporated. Mix in the molasses, then the fresh ginger and eggs. Mix in the flour mixture in 3 additions alternating with the espresso mixture in 2 additions. Distribute between 9 prepped molds. Scatter 2 teaspoons sugar over. Let the cakes bake for 20 minutes till tester pricked close the middle comes out clean. Allow the cakes to cool in pans for 10 minutes; transfer onto baking sheet. Can be prepared 6 hours in advance; allow to sit at room temperature. Reheat for 8 minutes in 350°F oven. Serve the ginger cakes while warm together with warm apricot sauce.

Nutrition Information

- Calories: 711
- Protein: 6 g(12%)
- Total Fat: 27 g(41%)
- Saturated Fat: 15 g(73%)
- Sodium: 464 mg(19%)
- Fiber: 2 g(8%)
- Total Carbohydrate: 115 g(38%)
- Cholesterol: 105 mg(35%)

49. Johnnycake Bread

Serving: Makes 8 servings | Prep: | Ready in:

Ingredients

- 1/4 cup vegetable oil, plus more for pans
- 1 1/4 cups all-purpose flour
- 3/4 cup cornmeal

- 1/4 cup granulated sugar
- 1 1/2 teaspoon baking powder
- 3/4 teaspoon kosher salt
- 2 large eggs
- 1 cup whole milk
- 1/4 cup mild-flavored (light) molasses
- 1 tablespoon maple sugar or raw sugar

Direction

- Heat an oven to 325°F. Oil 1 8 1/2x4 1/2-in. loaf pan or 2 5x2 1/2-in. loaf pans lightly. Whisk salt, baking powder, granulated sugar, cornmeal and flour in a big bowl. Create well in middle; add 1/4 cup oil, milk, molasses and eggs. Whisk in the dry ingredients. Divide batter among pans; sprinkle maple sugar.
- Bake breads for 50-55 minutes for big loaf or 40-45 minutes for small loves till inserted tester in middle exits clean and golden. Put pans on wire rack; cool breads prior to turning out for 10 minutes.
- You can make breads 1 day ahead; keep tightly wrapped at room temperature.

Nutrition Information

- Calories: 285
- Saturated Fat: 1 g(7%)
- Sodium: 241 mg(10%)
- Fiber: 1 g(4%)
- Total Carbohydrate: 44 g(15%)
- Cholesterol: 50 mg(17%)
- Protein: 6 g(11%)
- Total Fat: 10 g(15%)

50. Kentucky Gingerbread

Serving: | Prep: | Ready in:

Ingredients

- 1 stick (1/2 cup) unsalted butter
- 1/2 cup vegetable shortening
- 3 large eggs
- 1 cup sugar
- 1 cup unsulfured molasses
- 1 teaspoon ground ginger
- 1 teaspoon ground cinnamon
- 1/2 teaspoon ground cloves
- 1/4 teaspoon salt
- 1 teaspoon baking soda
- 1 tablespoon warm water
- 2 cups all-purpose flour
- 1 cup boiling water
- Accompaniment: whipped cream

Direction

- Preheat an oven to 350°F. Oil and flour a square 9×2-inch baking pan, shaking off extra flour.
- Over medium-low heat, liquify the shortening and butter in a saucepan and take pan off heat. Mix together salt, spices, molasses, sugar and eggs in a big bowl and in a slow stream, put the butter mixture, mixing. Dissolve baking soda with warm water in a cup and mix into the batter. Sift the flour on top of batter and mix till incorporated thoroughly. In a slow stream, pour boiling water, mixing, and put the batter into the baking pan.
- In center of the oven, bake the gingerbread for 45 minutes, or till a tester gets out clean. Allow the gingerbread to cool in pan on a rack.
- Slice the gingerbread into squares and serve at room temperature or while warm along with whipped cream.

Nutrition Information

- Calories: 288
- Saturated Fat: 6 g(28%)
- Sodium: 138 mg(6%)
- Fiber: 1 g(2%)
- Total Carbohydrate: 40 g(13%)
- Cholesterol: 50 mg(17%)
- Protein: 3 g(6%)
- Total Fat: 13 g(20%)

51. Lamb Köfte With Yogurt Sauce And Muhammara

Serving: Makes 6 servings | Prep: | Ready in:

Ingredients

- 1 cup plain low-fat yogurt
- 2 tablespoons tahini (sesame seed paste)*
- 1 tablespoon fresh lemon juice
- 1/2 teaspoon salt
- 2 pounds ground lamb
- 1/2 cup minced fresh mint
- 1/4 cup coarsely grated onion
- 4 garlic cloves, minced
- 3 tablespoons paprika
- 1 tablespoon ground cumin
- 1 1/2 teaspoons coarse kosher salt
- 1 teaspoon freshly ground black pepper
- 1/2 teaspoon cayenne pepper
- 12 5-to 7-inch-diameter soft round Middle Eastern flatbreads (preferably with no pocket)
- 2 tablespoons (or more) olive oil, divided
- 2 large onions, halved through core, cut crosswise into 1/4- to 1/3-inch slices
- 1/2 cup finely chopped drained roasted red peppers from jar
- 1/2 cup water
- 2 tablespoons (or more) pomegranate molasses**
- 2 tablespoons chopped fresh Italian parsley

Direction

- For yogurt sauce: in medium bowl, mix every ingredient to incorporate. Put on a cover and refrigerate.
- For the Köfte: with plastic wrap, line big rimmed baking sheet. In big bowl, slowly combine lamb and following 8 ingredients. With scant 2 tablespoonfuls for each, roll the meat mixture forming 1 1/2-inch meatballs using moistened hands. Set on the sheet.
- Preheat an oven to 300°F. On work area, put big sheet of foil. Over moderately-high heat, heat big nonstick or cast-iron skillet. In skillet, put the flatbreads one by one; cook for 2 minutes on each side till browned. Wrap in foil; put into oven to retain warmth.
- In the same skillet, heat a tablespoon oil over moderately-high heat. Put in the onions; lightly scatter pepper and salt on top. Sauté for 8 minutes till golden brown.
- Move onions to 1 side of big rimmed baking sheet; put into the oven to retain warmth.
- In the same skillet, put a tablespoon of oil; heat over moderately-high heat. Sauté 1/2 of meatballs for 7 to 8 minutes till just cooked through. Transfer to baking sheet in the oven. Redo with the rest of meatballs, putting oil into skillet if dry. Set skillet aside.
- For muhammara: In reserved skillet, put the roasted peppers; mix for a minute. Put in 2 tablespoons pomegranate molasses and half-cup water. Bring to a simmer, scratching up browned bits. Cook for 4 minutes till cooked down to 2/3 cup, mixing from time to time. Stir in parsley. Season with pepper, salt to taste and additional pomegranate molasses, if wished. Move to a small bowl.
- On a platter, set meatballs and onions. Serve along with muhammara, yogurt sauce and warm breads.

Nutrition Information

52. Lemon Molasses Chess Pie

Serving: Serves 8 to 10 | Prep: | Ready in:

Ingredients

- pastry dough
- pie weights or raw rice for weighting shell
- 2 lemons
- 1/2 stick (1/4 cup) unsalted butter
- 4 large eggs
- 1 1/4 cups sugar

- 1/4 cup unsulfured molasses
- 1/4 cup heavy cream
- 2 tablespoons yellow cornmeal
- 1/8 teaspoon salt
- Accompaniment: lightly sweetened whipped cream

Direction

- Using a floured rolling pin, roll out dough into 1/8-inch thick, approximately a 12-inch round on a slightly floured surface. Fit the dough into a glass 9-inch or 1-quart pie plate and clip the edge. Flute the edge of shell in a decorative manner and using a fork puncture the base of shell in few areas. Refrigerate the shell for half an hour, or till set.
- Preheat the oven to 375°F.
- With foil, line the shell and fill with raw rice or pie weights. Allow the shell to bake in center of the oven for 25 minutes. To a rack, put the shell and cautiously take off rice or weights and the foil. Let the shell cool.
- Raise the temperature to 450°F. From lemons, finely grate sufficient zest to get a tablespoon and juice the lemons to measure 3 tablespoons. Liquify the butter and allow to cool. Beat together sugar and eggs in a bowl with electric mixer till pale and thick and beat in lemon juice, zest, butter and every leftover ingredient on moderate speed till incorporated. The custard will be thin. Put the custard into the shell.
- In center of the oven, place the pie and lower the temperature to 325°F. Let the pie bake for 35 to 40 minutes till barely set in middle, and allow to cool fully on rack. Pie may be prepared for 6 hours in advance and store without a cover, at cool room temperature.
- At room temperature, serve the pie together with whipped cream.

Nutrition Information

53. Lemon, Blueberry, And Gingerbread Trifles

Serving: Serves 8 | Prep: | Ready in:

Ingredients

- 1 1/2 cups all-purpose flour
- 1 teaspoon baking soda
- 1/4 teaspoon salt
- 1 teaspoon ground ginger
- 1 teaspoon ground cinnamon
- 1/8 teaspoon ground cloves
- 1/4 teaspoon ground allspice
- 1/2 stick (1/4 cup) unsalted butter, softened
- 1/2 cup sugar
- 1/3 cup unsulfured molasses
- 2 tablespoons vegetable oil
- 2 large eggs
- 1 1/2 pounds frozen blueberries (about 5 cups)
- 3/4 cup sugar
- 1/2 cup water
- 1 tablespoon fresh lemon juice
- 8 large egg yolks
- 1 cup sugar
- 3/4 cup fresh lemon juice (from about 3 large lemons)
- 7 tablespoons unsalted butter, cut into pieces and softened
- 1 tablespoon freshly grated lemon zest (from about 2 large lemons)
- 1 cup well-chilled heavy cream
- Garnish: fresh lemon zest, removed with a vegetable peeler and cut into julienne strips

Direction

- Gingerbread: Preheat an oven to 350°F: line wax paper on buttered 15 1/2 x 10 1/2 x 1-in. jellyroll pan. Butter then flour paper; knock excess flour out.
- Mix spices, salt, baking soda and flour in a bowl. Use electric mixer to beat oil, molasses, sugar and butter till well combined in a big bowl; one by one, beat in eggs, beating well after each. Add flour mixture; beat till batter is well combined.

- Evenly spread batter in prepped pan; bake for 15 minutes or till lightly pressing it makes it spring back in middle of oven. Invert gingerbread on rack; fully cool. Peel wax paper off. You can make gingerbread 1 day ahead, kept wrapped in plastic wrap. Slice gingerbread to 1/2-in. cubes.
- Blueberry sauce: Simmer sauce ingredients in a small saucepan for 40-45 minutes or till reduced to 2 1/2 cups, occasionally mixing. Fully cool sauce; chill, covered. You can make it 2 days ahead, covered, chilled.
- Lemon mousse: Whisk sugar and yolks in a heavy saucepan. Add butter and lemon juice; cook on medium low heat till butter fully melts, constantly whisking. Cook for 7-12 minutes longer till its thick and just reaches boiling point, don't boil, whisking constantly.
- Strain lemon mixture through fine sieve into a bowl; mix in zest. Fully cool, surface covered using plastic wrap. Chill for 2 hours till cold.
- Use electric mixer to beat cream just till it holds stiff peaks in a bowl; whisk 1/4 whipped cream into the lemon mixture to lighten it. Gently yet thoroughly fold in leftover cream; chill mousse for 3 hours minimum or overnight, covered. You can make mousse 2 days ahead, covered, chilled.
- In bottom of each 8 1 1/2-cup capacity glasses, put 1/2 cup gingerbread cubes. Put 1/4 cup mousse on gingerbread in every glass; put 2 heaping tbsp. sauce on each mousse layer. Repeat layers with all but blueberry sauce, leftover mousse and 1 cup gingerbread. Otherwise, you can layer ingredients in the same order in a 3-qt. bowl to make a big trifle.
- Chill trifle for 6 hours minimum or overnight, covered; garnish trifle with zest.

Nutrition Information

- Calories: 750
- Saturated Fat: 19 g(96%)
- Sodium: 278 mg(12%)
- Fiber: 3 g(13%)
- Total Carbohydrate: 102 g(34%)
- Cholesterol: 314 mg(105%)
- Protein: 8 g(17%)
- Total Fat: 37 g(56%)

54. Licorice Pudding

Serving: Makes 6 servings | Prep: 20mins | Ready in:

Ingredients

- 3/4 cup very finely chopped Panda brand black licorice sticks or pieces (3 3/8 ounces)
- 1/4 teaspoon salt
- 4 1/2 cups whole milk
- 1/3 cup plus 2 1/2 tablespoons sugar
- 1 tablespoon plus 2 teaspoons cornstarch
- 3 large egg yolks
- 1 1/2 tablespoons unsalted butter
- Accompaniment: almond cakes
- an instant-read thermometer

Direction

- In a 2- to 3-quart heavy saucepan, mix 1/3 cup sugar, 4 cups milk, salt and licorice and heat over medium-low heat. Do not allow it to boil, mixing often, till licorice is dissolved, around 18 to 20 minutes. In case licorice is not fully dissolved, allow the mixture sit off heat, without a cover, mixing from time to time for 10 minutes.
- Raise the heat to medium and bring the milk mixture to a bare simmer.
- In a small bowl, mix together the leftover 1/2 cup milk and cornstarch.
- Mix the cornstarch mixture into the licorice mixture, and simmer for 2 minutes to thicken, mixing.
- In a medium bowl, mix together the leftover 2 1/2 tablespoons sugar and egg yolks till well blended, then put hot milk mixture in a slow stream into the bowl, mixing. Put back into saucepan and cook over medium heat, mixing continuously, till thermometer reads 170°F.

- Quickly pour through a fine-mesh sieve into a clean bowl, and mix in butter till combined.
- Refrigerate the pudding for 4 hours, covered the top with a round of wax paper, till really cold.
- Barely prior to serving, slowly mix the pudding, then distribute into 6 glasses or bowls.
- Serve together with almond cakes.
- Note: pudding can be refrigerated in bowl while the top of pudding is covered with wax paper and the bowl is covered with plastic wrap after 4 hours up to 3 days.

Nutrition Information

- Sodium: 68 mg(3%)
- Fiber: 0 g(1%)
- Total Carbohydrate: 6 g(2%)
- Protein: 0 g(0%)
- Total Fat: 10 g(16%)
- Saturated Fat: 1 g(7%)

56. Molasses Barbecue Sauce

Serving: Makes 1 1/2 cups | Prep: | Ready in:

Ingredients

- 3 cups chicken stock or canned low-salt chicken broth
- 1 cup dry white wine
- 1/4 cup apple cider vinegar
- 1/4 cup mild-flavored (light) molasses
- 1/4 cup chopped fresh tomato
- 3 tablespoons minced shallots
- 2 tablespoons chopped pitted dates
- 1 tablespoon chopped garlic
- 1/2 teaspoon dried crushed red pepper

Direction

- In a heavy big saucepan, mix every ingredient. Let boil for 20 minutes till cooked down to 1 1/2 cups, mixing from time to time. Season with pepper and salt to taste. Can be made a day in advance. Put a cover and refrigerate. Simmer prior to serving.

Nutrition Information

- Calories: 253
- Total Fat: 3 g(5%)
- Saturated Fat: 1 g(4%)
- Sodium: 360 mg(15%)
- Fiber: 1 g(5%)
- Total Carbohydrate: 41 g(14%)
- Cholesterol: 7 mg(2%)
- Protein: 7 g(14%)

55. Lime Molasses Vinaigrette

Serving: Makes 4 servings | Prep: 15mins | Ready in:

Ingredients

- 2 tablespoons fresh lime juice
- 4 teaspoons mild molasses
- 1/4 teaspoon hot sauce
- 1/2 teaspoon salt
- 3 tablespoons olive oil
- 1 scallion, finely chopped
- 1/4 teaspoon ground cumin
- Pinch of ground allspice

Direction

- In a bowl, mix together salt, hot sauce, molasses and lime juice.
- In a small skillet over medium heat, heat the oil together with spices and scallion till sizzling, then in a slow stream, put to the lime mixture, mixing till emulsified.

Nutrition Information

- Calories: 114

57. Molasses Crinkles

Serving: 48 | Prep: | Ready in:

Ingredients

- 3/4 cup shortening
- 1 cup packed brown sugar
- 1 egg
- 1/4 cup molasses
- 2 1/4 cups all-purpose flour
- 2 teaspoons baking soda
- 1/4 teaspoon salt
- 1/2 teaspoon ground cloves
- 1 teaspoon ground cinnamon
- 1 teaspoon ground ginger
- 1/3 cup granulated sugar for decoration

Direction

- Cream brown sugar and shortening. Mix in molasses and egg and combine thoroughly.
- Mix ginger, cinnamon, cloves, salt, baking soda and flour. To the shortening mixture, put flour mixture and combine thoroughly. Place a cover and refrigerate dough for a minimum of 2 to 3 hours.
- Preheat the oven to 175°C or 350°F. Oil the cookie sheets.
- Roll dough forming rounds to the size of big walnuts. Roll rounds in sugar and on the prepped baking sheets, set 3-inch away. Allow to bake for 10 to 12 minutes in the preheated oven. Allow to cool for a minute prior to putting to a wire rack to keep cooling.

Nutrition Information

- Calories: 79 calories;
- Protein: 0.7
- Total Fat: 3.4
- Sodium: 68
- Total Carbohydrate: 11.7
- Cholesterol: 4

58. Molasses Ice Cream

Serving: Makes about 1 quart | Prep: 10mins | Ready in:

Ingredients

- 3 oz cream cheese, softened
- 1/2 cup packed light brown sugar
- 1/3 cup mild molasses
- 2 cups half-and-half

Direction

- Blend molasses, brown sugar and cream cheese till smooth in a blender or food processor. Add half and half as motor runs, blending till combined.
- Freeze in ice cream maker. Put ice cream in an airtight container; to harden, put in freezer.

Nutrition Information

- Calories: 208
- Total Carbohydrate: 27 g(9%)
- Cholesterol: 34 mg(11%)
- Protein: 2 g(5%)
- Total Fat: 11 g(16%)
- Saturated Fat: 6 g(32%)
- Sodium: 73 mg(3%)

59. Molasses And Oat Soda Bread

Serving: Makes 2 loaves | Prep: | Ready in:

Ingredients

- Yellow cornmeal
- 1 1/4 cups buttermilk
- 1/4 cup mild-flavored (light) molasses
- 2 tablespoons vegetable oil
- 1 1/2 cups old-fashioned oats
- 3 cups unbleached all purpose flour
- 1/2 cup whole wheat flour

- 1 tablespoon sugar
- 1 1/2 teaspoons salt
- 1 teaspoon baking soda
- 1 teaspoon baking powder
- 1 cup raisins

Direction

- Preheat the oven to 400°F. Slightly grease a big baking sheet; scatter cornmeal over. In a medium bowl, mix oil, molasses and buttermilk. Mix in the oats; reserve. In a big bowl, combine the following 6 ingredients. Create a well in middle. Put the raisins and buttermilk mixture. Mix till dough gathers together, it will become moist. Allow to sit for 5 minutes.
- Slightly flour a work area. Onto the floured area, spoon 1/2 of dough; knead softly for 30 seconds barely till not sticky anymore. Form into 4 1/2-inch-diameter round. Redo with the leftover dough. On baking sheet, put the loaves, setting apart evenly. Create 2 parallel shallow cut on top of each loaf with a sharp serrated knife, approximately 3/4 inch deep.
- Let the loaves bake for 20 minutes. Lower heat to 375°F. Allow to bake for 25 minutes till crusty and dark and loaves sound empty once tapped on bottom. Put the loaves to a rack; cool fully. Can be prepared 8 hours in advance.

Nutrition Information

- Calories: 311
- Cholesterol: 1 mg(0%)
- Protein: 8 g(16%)
- Total Fat: 4 g(7%)
- Saturated Fat: 1 g(3%)
- Sodium: 265 mg(11%)
- Fiber: 3 g(13%)
- Total Carbohydrate: 62 g(21%)

60. Molasses, Rum, And Ginger Milk Punch

Serving: Makes about 8 cups. | Prep: | Ready in:

Ingredients

- 3/4 cup unsulfured molasses
- 2 teaspoons ground ginger, or to taste
- 4 cups chilled milk
- 2 cups chilled half-and-half
- 1 cup light rum
- 1/2 cup brandy
- Garnish: freshly grated nutmeg for sprinkling the punch

Direction

- Beat together the ginger and molasses in a punch bowl, beat in brandy, rum, half-and-half and milk, and refrigerate the punch with a cover for a minimum of 4 hours, or till it is extremely cold. Transfer the punch in punch glasses and scatter nutmeg over then serve.

Nutrition Information

- Calories: 274
- Sodium: 72 mg(3%)
- Fiber: 0 g(0%)
- Total Carbohydrate: 26 g(9%)
- Cholesterol: 28 mg(9%)
- Protein: 5 g(9%)
- Total Fat: 9 g(14%)
- Saturated Fat: 5 g(26%)

61. Molasses Baked Onions

Serving: Makes 8 side-dish servings | Prep: 30mins | Ready in:

Ingredients

- 4 large sweet onions such as Vidalia, Walla Walla, or Oso Sweet (3 to 4 lb total)

- 1 1/2 cups tomato juice (12 fluid ounces)
- 1 1/2 cups water
- 2 tablespoons unsalted butter
- 2 tablespoons molasses (regular or robust; not blackstrap)
- 1/2 teaspoon salt, or to taste
- 8 bacon slices (1/2 pound), halved crosswise

Direction

- Set the oven rack in center place and preheat the oven to 400°F.
- Remove skin and clip the onions, retaining root ends attach, then cut each in half lengthwise. In a 13×9×2-inch glass baking dish or another 2 1/2-quart shallow baking dish, lay in a single layer cut sides facing up.
- In a 2-quart heavy saucepan, boil salt, molasses, butter, water and tomato juice, mixing from time to time, then put on top of onions. Let the onions bake without a cover for 2 hours, basting with juices every 30 minutes, till soft.
- On top of every onion half, drape 2 pieces of bacon side by side and keep baking the onions for an hour longer, basting one time with juices midway through baking, till juices are thickened, bacon is browned and onions are extremely soft.

Nutrition Information

- Calories: 232
- Saturated Fat: 6 g(28%)
- Sodium: 358 mg(15%)
- Fiber: 2 g(8%)
- Total Carbohydrate: 21 g(7%)
- Cholesterol: 26 mg(9%)
- Protein: 6 g(11%)
- Total Fat: 14 g(22%)

62. Molasses Brined Turkey With Gingersnap Gravy

Serving: Makes 12 to 14 servings | Prep: | Ready in:

Ingredients

- 5 cups low-salt chicken broth
- 2 medium carrots, chopped
- 2 large celery stalks, chopped
- 1 onion, halved
- 2 small bay leaves
- Neck, heart, and gizzard reserved from 18- to 20-pound turkey
- 1 18- to 20-pound turkey
- 7 quarts water
- 2 cups coarse salt (about 9 ounces)
- 1 cup (packed) dark brown sugar
- 1 cup mild-flavored (light) molasses
- 2 bunches fresh thyme
- 1 bunch fresh sage
- 2 quarts ice cubes
- 2 large onions, halved
- 1 head of garlic, halved horizontally
- 3 tablespoons olive oil
- 1 tablespoon ground black pepper
- 1 tablespoon chopped fresh thyme
- 1 tablespoon chopped fresh sage
- 4 cups (about) low-salt chicken broth
- 1 cup finely chopped onion
- 1 tablespoon chopped fresh thyme
- 20 gingersnap cookies, coarsely crumbled (about 1 3/4 cups)
- 3 to 4 tablespoons apple cider vinegar
- 1 teaspoon Worcestershire sauce
- 1/4 cup whipping cream (optional)

Direction

- Stock: in a big saucepan, mix bay leaves, onion, celery, carrots and broth. Put the reserved gizzard, heart and neck. Boil; lower the heat to moderately-low and let simmer for an hour till stock is cooked down to 3 1/4 cups. Into medium bowl, filter the turkey stock. Can be prepared a day in advance. Cover the stock and chill.

- Brine and turkey: with 2 30-gallon plastic bags, line huge bowl approximately 16-quart, 1 inside the other one. Wash turkey outside and inside. In a bowl lined with plastic, put the turkey. In a big bowl or pot, mix the 1/2 bunch sage, 1 bunch thyme, molasses, sugar, salt and 7 quarts water. Mix till sugar and salt melt. Add in the ice cubes. Put the brine in the plastic bags on top of the turkey. Hold tops of bags together, getting rid of the air space over brine; enclose the bags. Chill the turkey for 18 to 20 hours in brine.
- At lowest place in oven, position the rack and preheat the oven to 350°F. Take turkey off brine. Drain extremely well; throw the brine. Pat the turkey dry outside and inside. On a small rack place in a big roasting pan, put the turkey. Stuff primary cavity with garlic, onions, 1/2 bunch sage and leftover 1 bunch thyme. In a small bowl, mix the chopped sage, chopped thyme, pepper and oil to create paste; coat the entire outer part of the turkey. Tuck the wing tips beneath; loosely bind the legs together to keep shape.
- Let the turkey roast for an hour, with foil, tenting loosely incase browning fast. Rotate the pan around; let the turkey roast for half an hour. Over the turkey, put a cup of broth; tent loosely once more with the foil. Allow the turkey to roast for 2 hours more, basting with a cup of broth every 30 minutes till thermometer pricked into chunkiest part of thigh reads 175°F. To a platter, put the turkey. Take herbs and vegetables off primary cavity and throw. Into the roasting pan, scoop any juices from the cavity. Allow turkey to rest for 30 minutes, inner temperature will raise for 5 to 10 degrees.
- Gravy: into bowl, filter the pan juices. Skim off fat, setting 2 tablespoons aside. In a heavy big saucepan, heat reserved 2 tablespoons of turkey fat over moderately-high heat. Put the thyme and onion. Sauté for 10 minutes till onion browns. Put the Worcestershire sauce, 3 tablespoons cider vinegar, gingersnaps and turkey stock. Put 2 cups defatted pan juices and boil, mixing to dissolve the gingersnaps. Lower the heat to moderately-low and allow to simmer for 4 minutes till gravy thickens. Season gravy with pepper and salt to taste, putting leftover tablespoon cream and vinegar, if wished.
- Serve turkey together with the gravy.

Nutrition Information

- Calories: 1028
- Fiber: 3 g(10%)
- Total Carbohydrate: 60 g(20%)
- Cholesterol: 367 mg(122%)
- Protein: 116 g(232%)
- Total Fat: 35 g(53%)
- Saturated Fat: 9 g(43%)
- Sodium: 4077 mg(170%)

63. Molasses Cured Pork Shoulder Bacon

Serving: Makes about 4 1/2 lbs | Prep: 1.25hours | Ready in:

Ingredients

- 1 (4- to 6-lb) boneless pork shoulder Boston roast (Boston butt)
- 6 cups water
- 1 cup kosher salt
- 2/3 cup packed dark brown sugar
- 2 1/2 tablespoons Instacure No. 1*
- 1/2 cup mild molasses
- 3 cups ice cubes
- 4 tablespoons coarsely ground black pepper (optional)
- 1- to 2-gallon plastic storage tub or stainless-steel bowl; a 221/2-inch covered kettle grill with a hinged top rack; a 12- by 8- by 2-inch disposable aluminum roasting pan; 3 lb hardwood sawdust*; charcoal briquettes; a chimney starter; long metal tongs; an instant-read thermometer

Direction

- On a work area, place the pork butt, fat side facing up, then slice in half horizontally using a sharp big knife.
- In storage tub, mix together Instacure, brown sugar, salt and water for 3 minutes till solids are dissolved, then put the molasses and mix till dissolved. Put the ice and mix till cure is cold, ice may not be fully melted; maintaining liquid cold slows salt intake.
- Put the pork to cure, then weight using a big plate to maintain soaked. Cover tub using plastic wrap or with a lid, refrigerate for 36 hours.
- Wash the pork and pat it dry, then throw the brine. Scatter pepper evenly on pork (optional).
- Have grill ready and smoke the bacon: using a sharp knife, slice the bacon crosswise making 1/8-inch thick pieces, then in a heavy skillet, fry over medium-low heat, flipping, till browned. Put to paper towels to let drain.

Nutrition Information

64. Molasses And Buttermilk Gingerbread Squares

Serving: Makes 16 servings | Prep: | Ready in:

Ingredients

- Nonstick vegetable oil spray
- 1 1/4 cups all purpose flour
- 2 teaspoons ground cinnamon
- 1 teaspoon ground ginger
- 1/2 teaspoon baking soda
- 1/8 teaspoon ground nutmeg
- 1/2 cup mild-flavored (light) molasses
- 1/2 cup sugar
- 1/2 cup (1 stick) unsalted butter, melted
- 1/2 cup buttermilk
- 1 large egg
- 1 tablespoon powdered sugar

Direction

- Preheat the oven to 325°F. With non-stick vegetable oil spray, coat a metal baking pan, 8x8x2-inch in size. Into a medium bowl, sift ground nutmeg, baking soda, ground ginger, ground cinnamon and all-purpose flour. In a big bowl, put together the large egg, buttermilk, liquified butter, half cup sugar and molasses; mix to incorporate. Mix in the dry ingredients. Put the batter into prepped baking pan.
- Allow the cake to bake for 25 minutes till tester pricked into middle comes out clean. Let the cake cool fully in pan on rack. On top of the cake, sift the powdered sugar. Slice cake into 16 cubes.

Nutrition Information

- Calories: 157
- Total Carbohydrate: 23 g(8%)
- Cholesterol: 27 mg(9%)
- Protein: 2 g(3%)
- Total Fat: 7 g(11%)
- Saturated Fat: 4 g(19%)
- Sodium: 63 mg(3%)
- Fiber: 0 g(2%)

65. Moravian Crisps With Royal Icing

Serving: Makes 40 to 80 cookies (Depending on size) | Prep: 1hours | Ready in:

Ingredients

- 1/4 cup vegetable shortening (trans-fat-free)
- 1/3 cup packed light brown sugar
- 1/2 cup unsulfured molasses (not blackstrap)
- 1 1/2 cups all-purpose flour

- 1 1/4 teaspoons baking soda
- 1 teaspoon ground cinnamon
- 1 teaspoon ground ginger
- 3/4 teaspoon ground cloves
- 1/4 teaspoon salt
- 1 (1-pound) box confectioners sugar
- 4 teaspoons powdered egg whites (not reconstituted) such as Just Whites
- 1/2 cup water
- 1 tablespoon fresh lemon juice
- 1 teaspoon pure vanilla extract
- Food coloring (optional)
- Equipment: a pastry or flour-sack cloth and a cloth rolling-pin sleeve; decorative cookie cutters; a small offset spatula; pastry bags fitted with pastry tips

Direction

- For cookies: in a food processor, pulse molasses, brown sugar and shortening till smooth. Meantime, beat together salt, spices, baking soda and flour. Put to processor and mix till incorporated.
- Onto a floured area, transfer the dough and knead briskly, letting dough to soak in a bit more flour in case it's sticky. Split dough in 2 parts and shape every 1/2 into a 3-inch cube. Using plastic wrap, wrap every dough and refrigerate for a minimum of 1 day.
- With rack in center, preheat an oven to 325°F. With parchment paper, line 2 big baking sheets.
- On a floured pastry cloth, roll out a portion of dough with floured rolling pin covered with sleeve till really thin, less than 1/16-inch thick approximately 15-inch square. Using cookie cutters, cut out forms and, with offset spatula transfer on baking sheets, set approximately half-inch away.
- Let the cookies bake for 10 minutes, one sheet at a time. On sheet, allow to sit for a minute, then loosen using spatula and to crisp, put to a rack on parchment for 10 minutes. Incase initial batch is not crisp, let bake on baking sheet for a minute longer, then bake the rest of batches for 10 to 11 minutes. Allow the cookies to cool fully on rack.
- Redo with the rest of the dough, let baking sheets cool and line with new parchment. Roll scraps once more for additional cookies if wished.
- For icing: in a big bowl using electric mixer, mix together the icing ingredients at moderate speed for a minute till just blended. Raise the speed to high and mix for 3 minutes longer till icing holds soft peaks. If wished, distribute the icing and put food coloring.
- With icing, fill the pastry bags and pipe on a decorative manner on cookies, then allow to set for 1 hour.

Nutrition Information

- Calories: 62
- Fiber: 0 g(0%)
- Total Carbohydrate: 13 g(4%)
- Protein: 0 g(1%)
- Total Fat: 1 g(1%)
- Saturated Fat: 0 g(1%)
- Sodium: 38 mg(2%)

66. Muscovy Duck Breasts With Pomegranate Wine Sauce

Serving: Makes 8 servings | Prep: | Ready in:

Ingredients

- 3 tablespoons olive oil, divided
- 1 1/2 cups minced shallots (about 8 large)
- 6 garlic cloves, minced
- 1 1/4 cups dry white wine, divided
- 3/4 cup dry red wine
- 2 14-ounce cans low-salt chicken broth
- 1 14-ounce can low-salt beef broth
- 3/4 cup fresh orange juice
- 2 tablespoons pomegranate molasses*
- 3 teaspoons minced fresh marjoram, divided
- 1 fresh bay leaf

- 4 pounds boneless Muscovy duck breasts (4 to 8 breast halves, depending on size)
- 1 1/2 tablespoons all purpose flour

Direction

- Put 2 tbsp. of oil in a heavy medium saucepan and heat it over medium heat. Add and sauté the shallots for about 18 minutes until golden brown. Add the garlic and sauté for 3 minutes. Add a 3/4 cup of red wine and a cup of white wine. Let the mixture boil for about 10 minutes until most of the liquid is evaporated. Add the orange juice, both broths, 1 tsp. of marjoram, bay leaf, and pomegranate molasses. Bring the mixture to a boil for about 20 minutes until it is reduced to 2 cups. Discard the bay leaf. Take note that the sauce can be prepared 3 days ahead. Keep it covered and chilled.
- Place the rack at the lowest position of the oven and preheat it to 450°F. Rub the duck breast's meat side with 2 tsp. of marjoram and 1 tbsp. of olive oil. Sprinkle the meat with salt and pepper. Working in batches, sear the breasts in a heavy large skillet over high heat, skin-side down, for about 8 minutes until the fat is rendered and the skin is browned.
- Arrange the duck breasts on a rimmed baking sheet, skin-side down. Drain all the fat from the skillet except for 1 1/2 tbsp.; reserve the skillet. Roast the duck for about 20 minutes until the inserted thermometer in its thickest part registers 145°F (medium-rare).
- In the meantime, simmer the sauce. Reheat the reserved duck fat in the skillet over medium heat. Stir in the flour for 1 minute. Whisk in sauce gradually.
- Place the duck breasts on a cutting board. Pour off all the fat from the baking sheet. Add a 1/4 cup of white wine into the baking sheet. Scrape any browned bits and add them into the sauce. Simmer the sauce for 3 minutes until the flavors are well-blended. Season the sauce with salt and pepper. Slice the duck breasts thinly. Distribute the slices among 8 plates. Drizzle slices with the sauce.

Nutrition Information

- Calories: 433
- Saturated Fat: 4 g(20%)
- Sodium: 265 mg(11%)
- Fiber: 1 g(5%)
- Total Carbohydrate: 16 g(5%)
- Cholesterol: 175 mg(58%)
- Protein: 49 g(98%)
- Total Fat: 15 g(24%)

67. Oatmeal And Prune Muffins

Serving: Makes 12 muffins | Prep: | Ready in:

Ingredients

- 1 cup all-purpose flour
- 1/4 cup sugar
- 1 1/2 teaspoons double-acting baking powder
- 1 teaspoon salt
- 1/2 teaspoon baking soda
- 1 1/3 cups quick-cooking rolled oats
- 1 cup chopped pitted prunes
- 1 cup buttermilk
- 1/2 stick (1/4 cup) unsalted butter, melted and cooled
- 1/4 cup unsulfured molasses
- 1 large egg, beaten lightly

Direction

- Sift together baking soda, salt, baking powder, sugar and flour in a bowl and mix in prunes and oats. Beat together egg, molasses, butter and buttermilk in a separate bowl, put the mixture to flour mixture, and mix batter till just blended. Distribute batter between a dozen well-buttered 1/3-cup muffin tins and let the muffins bake for 20 to 25 minutes in the center of a prepped 400°F oven, or till it springs back when touched and golden. Onto a rack, transfer the muffins and allow to cool.

Nutrition Information

- Calories: 191
- Cholesterol: 26 mg(9%)
- Protein: 4 g(8%)
- Total Fat: 5 g(8%)
- Saturated Fat: 3 g(14%)
- Sodium: 175 mg(7%)
- Fiber: 2 g(9%)
- Total Carbohydrate: 34 g(11%)

68. Old Fashioned Gingerbread

Serving: 12 | Prep: 15mins | Ready in:

Ingredients

- PAM® Baking Spray
- 2 3/4 cups Ultragrain® All Purpose Flour
- 1 tablespoon ground ginger
- 2 teaspoons ground cinnamon
- 2 teaspoons baking soda
- 1/2 teaspoon salt
- 1 cup firmly packed brown sugar
- 2/3 cup Pure Wesson® Vegetable Oil
- 2 large eggs, beaten
- 3/4 cup molasses
- 1 cup lowfat buttermilk
- 1 tablespoon confectioners' sugar
- Reddi-wip® Original Dairy Whipped Topping

Direction

- Set the oven to 350°F and start preheating. Coat a 13x9 inch baking dish with baking spray. In a medium bowl, combine salt, baking soda, cinnamon, ginger and flour; set aside.
- In a large bowl, combine eggs, oil and sugar; mix properly. Slowly add molasses to sugar mixture; stir until well incorporated. Add flour mixture alternately with buttermilk to sugar mixture; beat properly. Evenly distribute batter in prepared baking dish.
- Bake for 30 to 35 minutes in preheated oven until a wooden pick comes out clean after being inserted into the center. Cool for 10 minutes then cut into 12 smaller pieces. Dust with confectioner's sugar and add Reddi-whip on top to garnish. Serve.

Nutrition Information

- Calories: 359 calories;
- Protein: 5.7
- Total Fat: 14.1
- Sodium: 353
- Total Carbohydrate: 56.4
- Cholesterol: 32

69. Old Fashioned Gingerbread With Molasses Whipped Cream

Serving: Makes 8 to 10 servings | Prep: | Ready in:

Ingredients

- 1 cup plus 1 tablespoon sugar
- 1/2 cup (1 stick) unsalted butter, room temperature
- 3/4 cup plus 2 tablespoons mild-flavored (light) molasses
- 2 large eggs
- 2 cups all purpose flour
- 2 teaspoons baking soda
- 1 1/4 teaspoons ground cinnamon
- 3/4 teaspoon ground ginger
- 1/2 teaspoon salt
- 1 1/2 cups chilled whipping cream, divided
- 3/4 cup boiling water

Direction

- Preheat an oven to 350°F. Butter and flour a metal baking pan, 9x9x2-inch in size. In a big bowl, mix butter and 1 cup sugar with electric mixer till incorporated. Mix in 3/4 cup of the molasses, then the eggs one by one. Sift in salt,

ginger, cinnamon, baking soda and flour; mix till incorporated. Mix in quarter cup cream, then 3/4 cup of boiling water. Put the batter to prepped pan.
- Let the cake bake for 45 minutes till tester pricked into middle comes out clean. Allow the cake to cool in pan on rack.
- In a medium bowl, mix 1 tablespoon sugar and 1 1/4 cups cream till peaks create. Fold in 2 tablespoons of the molasses till streaks shows, avoid overmixing. Slice the cake into pieces; put to plates. Serve along with molasses whipped cream.

Nutrition Information

- Calories: 575
- Sodium: 442 mg(18%)
- Fiber: 1 g(4%)
- Total Carbohydrate: 80 g(27%)
- Cholesterol: 127 mg(42%)
- Protein: 6 g(12%)
- Total Fat: 27 g(41%)
- Saturated Fat: 16 g(82%)

70. Orange Molasses Bread

Serving: Serves 16 | Prep: | Ready in:

Ingredients

- 1 1/4 cups all purpose flour
- 1 1/4 cups whole wheat flour
- 1/2 cup yellow cornmeal
- 2 teaspoons baking powder
- 2 teaspoons grated orange peel
- 1 teaspoon aniseed, lightly crushed in mortar with pestle
- 3/4 teaspoon ground coriander
- 3/4 teaspoon salt
- 1/2 teaspoon baking soda
- 1 1/3 cups buttermilk
- 1/4 cup dark molasses
- 3 tablespoons canola oil
- 1 egg

Direction

- Preheat the oven to 350°F. Oil a glass loaf pan. In a big bowl, combine the initial 9 ingredients. In a separate bowl, mix egg, oil, molasses and buttermilk, and beat to incorporate. Put to the dry ingredients and mix till barely incorporated. Scoop into prepped pan. Allow to bake for 50 minutes till it springs back when touched. Let cool for 10 minutes in the pan on rack. Transfer onto rack and cool fully. Can be made a day in advance. Cover securely.

Nutrition Information

71. Peter Luger Style Steak Sauce

Serving: Makes about 1 1/2 cups | Prep: 10mins | Ready in:

Ingredients

- 1 cup ketchup
- 2 tablespoons plus 1 teaspoon Worcestershire sauce
- 2 tablespoons distilled white vinegar
- 2 tablespoons mild-flavored molasses
- 2 tablespoons prepared horseradish
- 1 tablespoon plus 1 teaspoon sugar
- 1/2 teaspoon garlic powder
- 1/4 teaspoon kosher salt
- 1/4 teaspoon freshly ground black pepper
- 1/4 teaspoon Louisiana-style hot sauce, such as Tabasco

Direction

- Whisk hot sauce, pepper, salt, garlic powder, sugar, horseradish, molasses, vinegar, Worcestershire and ketchup in medium bowl.
- You can make sauce 5 days ahead, stored in an airtight container and chilled.

Nutrition Information

- Calories: 160
- Total Fat: 0 g(0%)
- Saturated Fat: 0 g(0%)
- Sodium: 905 mg(38%)
- Fiber: 1 g(3%)
- Total Carbohydrate: 42 g(14%)
- Protein: 1 g(2%)

72. Pineapple Upside Down Pumpkin Gingerbread

Serving: Makes 10 servings | Prep: | Ready in:

Ingredients

- Nonstick vegetable oil spray
- 2/3 cup (packed) golden brown sugar
- 1/2 cup (1 stick) unsalted butter
- 2 tablespoons frozen pineapple juice concentrate, thawed
- 1 teaspoon mild-flavored (light) molasses
- 1 ripe pineapple, peeled
- 2 cups all purpose flour
- 2 teaspoons baking soda
- 2 teaspoons baking powder
- 1 1/4 teaspoons ground cinnamon
- 3/4 teaspoon ground ginger
- 1/2 teaspoon salt
- 1/2 cup (1 stick) unsalted butter, room temperature
- 1 cup sugar
- 2 large eggs
- 1/2 cup mild-flavored (light) molasses
- 1/2 cup canned pure pumpkin
- 1/2 cup boiling water
- Whipped cream

Direction

- Topping: preheat the oven to 350°F. With nonstick spray, coat a metal baking pan, 9x9x2-inch in size. In a heavy small saucepan, mix molasses, pineapple juice concentrate, butter and sugar. Boil over moderate heat, mixing till syrup is smooth and sugar dissolves; allow to boil for a minute. Evenly put into prepped pan.
- Slice off a 1/3-inch-thick circle from the pineapple; remove the core. In pan, put the circle in syrup. Let pineapple stand on end. Slice lengthwise making 1/3-inch-thick pieces. Cut out circles from slices of pineapple, with 3 round cutters of various sizes, avoiding the core. Set circles near each other in 1 layer in free-form design in syrup.
- Cake: in a medium bowl, mix the initial 6 ingredients. In a big bowl, whisk butter till fluffy. Put sugar and whisk to incorporate. Whisk in the eggs, one by one. Whisk in the molasses, then the pumpkin. Whisk in the dry ingredients barely till incorporated, scraping down sides of the bowl from time to time. Whisk in half cup of boiling water. Into the pan, put the batter evenly.
- Let the cake bake for 50 minutes till tester pricked into middle comes out clean. Allow the cake to cool in pan for 45 minutes. Put the platter on top of pan and flip. Allow to rest for 5 minutes. Carefully lift off pan. Serve cake at room temperature or while warm along with whipped cream.

Nutrition Information

- Calories: 533
- Fiber: 2 g(10%)
- Total Carbohydrate: 81 g(27%)
- Cholesterol: 86 mg(29%)
- Protein: 5 g(9%)
- Total Fat: 23 g(35%)
- Saturated Fat: 12 g(61%)
- Sodium: 471 mg(20%)

73. Pomegranate Cumin Dressing

Serving: Makes about 1 cup | Prep: 10mins | Ready in:

Ingredients

- 7 1/2 tablespoons extra-virgin olive oil
- 4 1/2 tablespoons white balsamic vinegar
- 3 tablespoons sliced fresh mint leaves
- 1 1/2 tablespoons pomegranate molasses
- 1 tablespoon ground cumin
- 6 tablespoons minced shallots
- ingredient info: If you can't find pomegranate molasses at the supermarket or a Middle Eastern store, make your own by boiling 1 cup pomegranate juice until reduced to 3 tablespoons syrup, about 15 minutes.

Direction

- In a bowl, mix the initial 5 ingredients. Add in the shallots; put pepper and salt to season.

Nutrition Information

74. Prune Armagnac Gingerbread

Serving: | Prep: | Ready in:

Ingredients

- unsweetened cocoa powder for dusting pan
- 1 cup chopped pitted prunes
- 1/2 cup Armagnac or Cognac
- 1 tablespoon minced peeled fresh gingerroot
- 3 cups all-purpose flour
- 2 teaspoons baking soda
- 2 teaspoons cinnamon
- 1 teaspoon ground ginger
- 1 teaspoon ground cloves
- 1/8 teaspoon cayenne
- 3/4 teaspoon salt
- 1 cup vegetable shortening at room temperature
- 1 1/2 cups packed light brown sugar
- 1 cup unsulfured molasses
- 1/2 cup strong brewed coffee
- 4 large eggs, beaten lightly
- 1 teaspoon vanilla
- 1/2 cup chopped crystallized ginger
- crème fraîche or sour cream for serving
- sliced kumquats for garnish

Direction

- Preheat the oven to 350°F. Butter a springform pan, 10-inch in size and dust with the cocoa powder, tapping excess out.
- Cook gingerroot, Armagnac and prunes in a skillet over medium-high heat, mixing often, till nearly all the liquid is evaporated. Take pan off heat.
- Sift salt, spices, baking soda and flour into a bowl. Cream the shortening in a separate bowl with electric mixer. Put the sugar, mixing, and beat the mixture till fluffy and light. In a stream, put the molasses, mixing till well incorporated. Mix in the vanilla, eggs, flour mixture and coffee till batter is just blended. At this point, it may separate. Set a tablespoon of crystallized ginger aside and into batter, mix the remaining together with prune mixture. Into prepped pan, transfer the batter and scatter reserved ginger on top.
- Let the gingerbread bake for 1 hour 20 minutes, or till a tester gets out clean, and let cool for an hour on a rack. Gingerbread will slightly sink in middle.
- Serve gingerbread at room temperature or while warm together with kumquats and crème fraîche.

Nutrition Information

- Calories: 339
- Saturated Fat: 3 g(15%)
- Sodium: 232 mg(10%)
- Fiber: 1 g(6%)
- Total Carbohydrate: 54 g(18%)
- Cholesterol: 37 mg(12%)
- Protein: 3 g(7%)

- Total Fat: 11 g(18%)

75. Pumpkin, Ginger And Molasses Tart

Serving: Makes 8 servings | Prep: | Ready in:

Ingredients

- 1 cup all purpose flour
- 1/2 cup cake flour
- 1/4 teaspoon salt
- 1/2 cup plus 2 tablespoons (1 1/4 sticks) unsalted butter, room temperature
- 1/4 cup sugar
- 1 large egg yolk
- 1/2 teaspoon vanilla extract
- 2 large eggs
- 1/2 cup (packed) dark brown sugar
- 2 tablespoons mild-flavored (light) molasses
- 2/3 cup whipping cream
- 1 teaspoon ground cinnamon
- 1/2 teaspoon ground ginger
- 1/8 teaspoon ground cloves
- 1/8 teaspoon salt
- 1 1/2 cups canned pure pumpkin
- 1 cup chilled whipping cream
- 2 tablespoons powdered sugar
- 1 teaspoon vanilla extract

Direction

- Crust: Whisk salt and both flours in a bowl. Beat sugar and butter with electric mixer till well blended in another bowl; beat in vanilla and yolk. Add flour mixture; beat till moist clumps form. Bring dough into a ball then flatten to disk; wrap in plastic then chill for 30 minutes.
- Put rack on bottom third of oven; preheat to 375°F. Roll dough disk to 12-in. round between 2 waxed paper or parchment paper sheets. Remove top parchment sheet; invert dough to 9-in. diameter tart pan that has removable bottom. Remove leftover parchment gently. Evenly press dough into pan; if needed, patch any tears in crust. Trim dough; leave 3/4-in. overhang. Press the overhang in to make double-thick sides. Use fork to pierce the bottom of dough all over. Put tart pan onto baking sheet. Bring dough scraps into ball; roll to 1/4-in. thick on a floured surface. Cut leaf shapes out with knife or small leaf-shaped cookie cutter. Put leaves onto baking sheet with the tart crust.
- Bake leaves for 10 minutes till light golden; put leaves on rack. Bake crust for 20 more minutes till edges start to brown; keep the tart pan on the baking sheet.
- Filling: Whisk molasses, brown sugar and eggs till smooth in a medium bowl; whisk in salt, cloves, ginger, cinnamon and whipping cream. Add pumpkin; whisk till blended well. Put into warm crust; bake the tart on a baking sheet for 45 minutes till edges of filling start to puff and are firm and filling is set on middle. Put tart on rack; cool thoroughly in the pan on a rack. You can make this 1 day ahead. Chill till cold; cover and keep refrigerated. Put pastry leaves over tart.
- Sweetened whipped cream: Beat vanilla, sugar and whipping cream till peaks form in a big bowl.
- Slice tart to wedges. Put whipped cream on top; serve.

Nutrition Information

- Calories: 503
- Total Fat: 32 g(49%)
- Saturated Fat: 19 g(97%)
- Sodium: 155 mg(6%)
- Fiber: 2 g(8%)
- Total Carbohydrate: 50 g(17%)
- Cholesterol: 163 mg(54%)
- Protein: 6 g(12%)

76. Raisin Ginger Breads

Serving: Makes 5 small loaves | Prep: | Ready in:

Ingredients

- 3 cups all-purpose flour
- 1 1/2 teaspoons baking soda
- 3/4 teaspoon salt
- 1 tablespoon ground ginger
- 2 teaspoons cinnamon
- 1 1/2 sticks (3/4 cup) unsalted butter, softened
- 3/4 cup firmly pack dark brown sugar
- 3 large eggs
- 1 cup sour cream
- 3/4 cup dark molasses
- 2 cups raisins

Direction

- Sift together the cinnamon, ginger, salt, baking soda and flour in a bowl. Cream brown sugar and butter in a big bowl with electric mixer and mix in eggs, one by one. Beat together the molasses and sour cream in a small bowl. Put flour mixture alternately with molasses mixture into butter mixture, starting and finishing with flour mixture and whisking the batter after each addition till just incorporated, and mix in raisins. Distribute the batter between 5 buttered and floured loaf pans, each 5 3/4×3 1/4×2-inches, and let bake breads for 35 to 40 minutes in the center of a preheated 350°F oven, till a tester gets out clean. Take the breads out of the pans and allow them to cool on a rack, right sides facing up. The breads keep wrapped firmly in plastic wrap and in foil, refrigerated for a week or frozen, for a month.

Nutrition Information

- Calories: 1057
- Protein: 15 g(29%)
- Total Fat: 41 g(63%)
- Saturated Fat: 24 g(120%)
- Sodium: 741 mg(31%)
- Fiber: 5 g(19%)
- Total Carbohydrate: 165 g(55%)
- Cholesterol: 209 mg(70%)

77. Real Gingerbread

Serving: Makes 9 squares | Prep: 30mins | Ready in:

Ingredients

- 2 1/4 cups all-purpose flour
- 1 teaspoon baking soda
- 1 teaspoon ground cinnamon
- 1/4 teaspoon ground allspice
- 1/2 teaspoon salt
- 1 stick (1/2 cup) unsalted butter, well softened
- 2/3 cup molasses (not blackstrap)
- 2/3 cup packed dark brown sugar
- 2 large eggs
- 3 tablespoons finely grated (with a rasp) peeled fresh ginger
- 2/3 cup hot water

Direction

- In center of the oven, set the oven rack and preheat the oven to 350°F. Grease a 9-inch square baking pan with butter.
- In a bowl, beat together salt, spices, baking soda and flour.
- In a big bowl, mix together ginger, eggs, brown sugar, molasses and butter using an electric mixer at moderate speed till blended. Lower the speed to low and stir in flour mixture till smooth, then put in hot water and stir till incorporated, batter may look curdled.
- In the pan, put the batter and bake for 35 to 40 minutes till a wooden skewer or pick pricked in middle of cake comes out clean. Let cool in pan on a rack to warm.

Nutrition Information

- Calories: 357

- Protein: 5 g(10%)
- Total Fat: 12 g(18%)
- Saturated Fat: 7 g(34%)
- Sodium: 271 mg(11%)
- Fiber: 1 g(4%)
- Total Carbohydrate: 59 g(20%)
- Cholesterol: 68 mg(23%)

78. Rich And Sticky Gingerbread With Marmalade

Serving: Makes 18 pieces | Prep: | Ready in:

Ingredients

- 1 2/3 cups self-rising flour
- 1 1/2 teaspoons ground ginger
- 1/2 cup (1 stick) unsalted butter, room temperature
- 3/4 cup robust-flavored (dark) molasses
- 2 large eggs
- 1 cup orange marmalade
- 1/2 cup golden raisins
- 1/3 cup chopped crystallized ginger (about 2 ounces)

Direction

- Preheat an oven to 325°F. Butter then flour 9x9x2-in. metal baking pan; use parchment paper to line bottom.
- Sift ground ginger and flour in a medium bowl. Use electric mixer to beat butter till fluffy in a big bowl; beat in molasses. In 3 additions, beat in flour mixture alternately with eggs, one by one. Beat in marmalade then crystallized ginger and raisins; put in prepped baking pan.
- Bake cake for 38 minutes till inserted tester in middle exits clean; fully cool cake in pan on rack. You can make this 1 day ahead, standing at room temperature, covered.
- Slice cake to 9 squares; halve each square to make 18 1 1/2x3-in. pieces.

Nutrition Information

- Calories: 201
- Cholesterol: 34 mg(11%)
- Protein: 2 g(4%)
- Total Fat: 6 g(9%)
- Saturated Fat: 3 g(17%)
- Sodium: 165 mg(7%)
- Fiber: 1 g(3%)
- Total Carbohydrate: 37 g(12%)

79. Scandinavian Spiced Christmas Cake With Applesauce Filling

Serving: Serves 8 | Prep: | Ready in:

Ingredients

- 1 1/2 cups all purpose flour
- 1/2 teaspoon ground ginger
- 1/2 teaspoon ground mace
- 1/2 teaspoon ground cardamom
- 1/4 teaspoon salt
- 1/2 teaspoon baking soda
- 1/4 cup water
- 1/2 cup solid vegetable shortening, room temperature
- 1 cup sugar
- 1 large egg
- 1/2 cup mild-flavored (light) molasses
- 1/2 cup buttermilk
- 1 1/4 cups applesauce
- 1/4 cup (packed) golden brown sugar
- 1/4 cup (1/2 stick) unsalted butter
- 1 cinnamon stick
- 3 cups chilled whipping cream
- 1/4 cup (packed) golden brown sugar
- 3 tablespoons mild-flavored (light) molasses
- 2 tablespoons brandy
- 1 1/2 cups sliced almonds, toasted

Direction

- To make cake: preheat the oven to 350°F. Slightly butter a 9-inch diameter and 2-inch

high sides cake pan. With parchment paper, line base of the pan. In a medium bowl, combine the initial 5 ingredients. In quarter cup water, dissolve baking soda.
- Beat sugar and shortening in a big bowl with electric mixer till incorporated. Mix in the egg. Slowly mix in the molasses. Add in the dry ingredients alternating with the buttermilk. Mix in the baking soda mixture. Put the batter to prepped pan. Allow to bake for 40 minutes till tester pricked into middle comes out clean. Put the pan to rack and let the cake cool for 10 minutes. To loosen the cake, slice around the sides of pan. Invert the cake onto rack; remove the paper. Cool fully.
- For the filling: in a heavy medium saucepan, mix every ingredient. Let cook over moderately-low heat for 20 minutes till thick and cooked down to a cup, mixing from time to time. Put the filling to a small bowl and cool fully. Throw cinnamon stick. Filling and cake can be made a day in advance. Put a cover on cake and allow to sit at room temperature. Cover the filling using plastic wrap and chill.
- To make frosting: in a big bowl, whisk brandy, 2 tablespoons molasses, sugar and chilled cream till stiff peaks create. Into the pastry bag equipped with medium star tip, scoop 3/4 cup of frosting.
- Slice the cake into 3 even layers. Put 1 cake layer to platter with tart pan bottom as support, cut side facing up. Scatter half cup applesauce filling on top. Scatter a cup of frosting on top. Redo the layering with one cake layer, half cup filling and a cup frosting. Put leftover cake layer on top, cut side facing down. Thinly over the top and sides of cake, scatter some of the leftover frosting. Onto cake sides, push almonds. Over the top of cake, sprinkle leftover 1 tablespoon molasses. Around the top edge of cake, pipe the rest of the frosting. Place a cover and chill for a minimum of 1 hour or up to 6 hours.

Nutrition Information

- Calories: 883
- Sodium: 238 mg(10%)
- Fiber: 3 g(14%)
- Total Carbohydrate: 90 g(30%)
- Cholesterol: 139 mg(46%)
- Protein: 9 g(19%)
- Total Fat: 56 g(86%)
- Saturated Fat: 25 g(126%)

80. Sherry Vinegar And Molasses Glazed Carrots

Serving: Makes 10 servings | Prep: | Ready in:

Ingredients

- 6 tablespoons (3/4 stick) butter
- 3 pounds small carrots (5 to 6 inches long), peeled, trimmed
- 2 tablespoons mild-flavored (light) molasses, divided
- 1/2 teaspoon (or more) coarse kosher salt
- 6 tablespoons Sherry wine vinegar, divided
- 2 tablespoons chopped fresh Italian parsley, divided

Direction

- In heavy huge skillet or pot, liquify butter over moderately-high heat. Put in 1/2 teaspoon coarse salt, 1 tablespoon molasses and carrots; sauté for 1 minute till carrots are covered in butter mixture. Put in 4 tablespoons of Sherry wine vinegar and sufficient water to nearly cover the carrots, approximately 4 cups, and boil. Put on a cover and boil for 2 minutes. Remove cover and boil for 20 minutes till liquid is cooked down to syrup and carrots are soft, mixing frequently. Can be done 4 hours in advance. Allow to sit at room temperature.
- Put 2 tablespoons vinegar and the leftover 1 tablespoon molasses into carrots, and toss over moderately-high heat for 3 minutes till carrots are thickly covered in glaze and warmed through. Mix in a tablespoon parsley. Season

carrots with additional coarse salt and liberal amount of ground black pepper to taste. Move the carrots to big bowl; scatter leftover 1 tablespoon parsley on top and serve.

Nutrition Information

- Calories: 130
- Total Fat: 7 g(11%)
- Saturated Fat: 4 g(22%)
- Sodium: 191 mg(8%)
- Fiber: 4 g(15%)
- Total Carbohydrate: 16 g(5%)
- Cholesterol: 18 mg(6%)
- Protein: 1 g(3%)

81. Smoky Bean Salad With Molasses Dressing

Serving: Serves 4 to 6 | Prep: | Ready in:

Ingredients

- 2 cups dried Great Northern beans
- 1/4 cup Sherry wine vinegar
- 1 tablespoon yellow mustard seeds
- 1/4 cup finely chopped drained oil-packed sun-dried tomatoes
- 3 tablespoons mild-flavored (light) molasses
- 2 teaspoons finely chopped canned chipotle
- 1/3 cup olive oil
- 3/4 cup finely chopped red onion
- 1/4 cup minced fresh parsley
- Canned chipotle chilies_packed in adobo sauce are available at Latin American markets and some supermarkets._

Direction

- In a big bowl, put the beans. Put sufficient cold water to submerge by 2-inch. Allow to sit for a minimum of 4 hours or overnight.
- In a medium bowl, mix mustard seeds and vinegar. Allow to sit for a minimum of 1 hour and up to 4 hours.
- Let the beans drain. Put in a big saucepan. Put sufficient water to submerge the beans by 3-inch. Boil. Lower the heat; place a cover and allow to simmer for 50 minutes till soft. Let drain. Cool beans fully.
- Into the vinegar mixture, mix chipotle chilies, molasses and sun-dried tomatoes. Slowly mix in the oil. In a big bowl, mix parsley, red onion and beans. Put sufficient dressing to cover the salad. Season with pepper and salt to taste. Can be made 6 hours in advance. Put a cover and chill. Bring to room temperature prior to serving.

Nutrition Information

- Calories: 391
- Fiber: 8 g(31%)
- Total Carbohydrate: 44 g(15%)
- Protein: 11 g(22%)
- Total Fat: 20 g(31%)
- Saturated Fat: 3 g(14%)
- Sodium: 540 mg(23%)

82. Soft Ginger Cookies

Serving: Makes about 40 | Prep: | Ready in:

Ingredients

- 4 cups all purpose flour
- 1 cup sugar
- 2 teaspoons baking soda
- 2 teaspoons ground ginger
- 1 teaspoon ground nutmeg
- 1 teaspoon ground cinnamon
- 1 teaspoon ground cloves
- 1/2 teaspoon salt
- 1 cup robust (dark) molasses
- 1/2 cup pure vegetable shortening
- 1 large egg, beaten to blend

- 1/2 cup boiling water
- Additional sugar

Direction

- In big bowl, mix the initial 8 ingredients. Put in the egg, shortening and molasses. Mix with electric mixer till well combined. Mix in half-cup of boiling water. Refrigerate dough for an hour.
- Preheat the oven to 400°F. Roll refrigerated dough by liberal tablespoonfuls into balls. Roll in more sugar to cover. On ungreased baking sheets, put dough balls 2 inches apart. Bake for 12 minutes till cookies are cracked on top and puffed and tester pricked into middle comes out with a few moist crumbs adhered, prevent from overbaking. Turn cookies onto racks and let cool.

Nutrition Information

- Calories: 116
- Total Fat: 3 g(4%)
- Saturated Fat: 1 g(4%)
- Sodium: 78 mg(3%)
- Fiber: 0 g(2%)
- Total Carbohydrate: 21 g(7%)
- Cholesterol: 5 mg(2%)
- Protein: 1 g(3%)

83. Sour Cream Bran Muffins

Serving: Makes 12 muffins | Prep: | Ready in:

Ingredients

- 1 stick (1/2 cup) unsalted butter, softened
- 1/4 cup firmly packed light brown sugar
- 1 large egg, beaten lightly
- 1 cup sour cream
- 1/4 cup dark molasses
- 1/2 cup raisins
- 1 cup all-purpose flour
- 1 teaspoon baking soda
- 1/4 teaspoon salt
- 1 cup miller's bran (available at natural foods stores, specialty foods shops, and some supermarkets)

Direction

- Use electric mixer to cream brown sugar and butter till fluffy and light in a big bowl; beat in molasses, sour cream and egg. Mix in raisins. Whisk bran, salt, baking soda and flour in a bowl; add mixture to sour cream mixture. Mix batter till just combined and lumpy. Put batter in 12 1/3-cup well-buttered muffin tins; bake muffins in center of preheated 400°F oven till springy to touch and golden brown or for 15-20 minutes. Turn out muffins onto a rack; cool.

Nutrition Information

- Calories: 205
- Saturated Fat: 7 g(36%)
- Sodium: 142 mg(6%)
- Fiber: 1 g(2%)
- Total Carbohydrate: 23 g(8%)
- Cholesterol: 46 mg(15%)
- Protein: 2 g(5%)
- Total Fat: 12 g(18%)

84. Speculoos Buttons

Serving: Makes about 90 | Prep: | Ready in:

Ingredients

- 2 cups all-purpose flour
- 1 tablespoon ground cinnamon
- 3/4 teaspoon ground ginger
- 1/2 teaspoon fine sea salt
- 1/2 teaspoon freshly grated nutmeg
- 1/8 teaspoon ground cloves
- 1/2 cup (1 stick) unsalted butter, room temperature

- 1/2 cup (packed) light brown sugar
- 1/4 cup sugar
- 2 tablespoons mild-flavored (light) molasses
- 1 large egg, room temperature
- 1 teaspoon vanilla extract
- 1 large egg white
- Sanding or other decorative sugar
- 2 cups powdered sugar, sifted
- Sprinkles, colored sanding sugar, or dragées (optional)

Direction

- Cookies: Whisk initial 6 ingredients in a medium bowl; put aside. Use electric mixer to beat butter at medium speed for 2 minutes till smooth in a medium bowl. Add molasses and both sugars; beat for 3 minutes till mixture is creamy and smooth. Beat in vanilla and egg; mix for 2 minutes. Lower speed to low then add dry ingredients; stir to blend well.
- Scrape dough from bowl; divide to thirds. Roll each dough piece to 8-in. log with your palms; tightly wrap logs in parchment paper or plastic. Freeze for 3 hours minimum. After 1 hour, take logs from freezer then roll on counter for neater edges. You can make dough 2 months ahead, keep frozen.
- Put racks in bottom and top thirds of oven and preheat to 375°F. Line silicone baking mats or parchment paper on 3 baking sheets.
- Whisk egg white to loosen in a small bowl; brush all over a log lightly. Roll in or sprinkle sanding sugar. Slice sliver of dough off each end of log to create ends flat with long, slender knife; cut the log to 1/4-in. thick rounds. Put on 1 baking sheet, 1/2-in. apart; while cutting next log, put in freezer. It's best to bake while dough is cold. Repeat using leftover dough.
- Bake 2 cookie sheets, rotating sheets from front to back and top to bottom after 6 minutes, for 11-13 minutes till centers are nearly firm and tops are golden brown. Put cookies on wire racks; cool. Repeat using 3rd cookie sheet; you can bake cookies 2 days ahead; keep airtight at room temperature.
- Glaze: Mix 7 tsp. cold water and powdered sugar till very thick in a big mixing bowl; put 1/2 tsp. glaze on every button. Alternately, use glaze to fill a resealable plastic bag; in 1 corner, cut small hole. In an even circle, pipe glaze around edges of cookies then fill. Use sprinkles, dragees or colored sugar, if desired, to garnish. Stand on rack for 30 minutes minimum for glaze to set at room temperature. You can make cookies 5 days ahead; keep airtight at room temperature.

Nutrition Information

- Calories: 38
- Fiber: 0 g(1%)
- Total Carbohydrate: 7 g(2%)
- Cholesterol: 5 mg(2%)
- Protein: 0 g(1%)
- Total Fat: 1 g(2%)
- Saturated Fat: 1 g(3%)
- Sodium: 15 mg(1%)

85. Spice Cookies

Serving: 48 | Prep: 15mins | Ready in:

Ingredients

- 1 1/2 cups white sugar
- 1 cup butter
- 2 eggs
- 1 1/2 teaspoons ground cinnamon
- 1/2 teaspoon ground nutmeg
- 1/4 teaspoon ground cloves
- 4 cups all-purpose flour
- 1 cup dried currants
- 1 1/2 teaspoons baking soda
- 1 cup milk, or as needed

Direction

- Preheat an oven to 175 °C or 350 °F. Slightly oil 2 baking sheets.

- In a bowl, mix cloves, nutmeg, cinnamon, eggs, butter and sugar; mix using an electric mixer till creamy. In another bowl, mix together the baking soda, currants and flour. Mix into the butter mixture alternating with tablespoons of milk till flour is completely blended.
- On the prepped baking sheets, drop spoonsful of batter. Using a fork, gently push down. In case fork adheres, dip it in water or sugar.
- In the prepped oven, bake for 10 to 15 minutes till golden brown. Allow to rest for a minute on baking sheets prior to transferring to a wire rack to cool fully.

Nutrition Information

- Calories: 110 calories;
- Total Carbohydrate: 16.8
- Cholesterol: 18
- Protein: 1.7
- Total Fat: 4.3
- Sodium: 72

86. Spiced Pumpkin Pie

Serving: 8 | Prep: 5mins | Ready in:

Ingredients

- 2 cups pumpkin
- 1/2 cup egg substitute
- 1/2 cup brown sugar
- 1 tablespoon pumpkin pie spice
- 12 fluid ounces nonfat evaporated milk
- 1 (9 inch) unbaked pie crust

Direction

- Preheat the oven to 175°C or 350°F.
- Combine together the nonfat evaporated milk, pumpkin pie spice, brown sugar, egg substitute and pumpkin in a medium bowl.
- Put pumpkin mixture into the pie crust. In the prepped oven, bake for an hour till an inserted knife in the center comes out clean.

Nutrition Information

- Calories: 240 calories;
- Total Carbohydrate: 34.6
- Cholesterol: 2
- Protein: 8
- Total Fat: 8.4
- Sodium: 207

87. Spiced And Glazed Molasses Cookies

Serving: Raw sugar (for sprinkling) | Prep: | Ready in:

Ingredients

- 1 1/4 cups all-purpose flour
- 1/2 cup whole wheat flour
- 1 teaspoon baking soda
- 1 teaspoon kosher salt
- 2 teaspoons ground ginger
- 1 1/2 teaspoon ground cinnamon
- 1/2 teaspoon ground cloves
- 1 1/2 teaspoons finely ground black pepper, plus more for sprinkling
- 1 cup (packed) dark brown sugar
- 1/2 cup (1 stick) unsalted butter, room temperature
- 1 large egg, room temperature
- 1/3 cup plus 1 tablespoon mild-flavored (light) molasses
- 3/4 cup powdered sugar
- 1 tablespoon (or more) milk
- Raw sugar (for sprinkling)

Direction

- In a medium bowl, mix 1 1/2 teaspoon pepper, cloves, cinnamon, ginger, salt, baking

soda, whole wheat flour and all-purpose flour to blend.
- In a big bowl, beat butter and brown sugar with an electric mixer on moderate speed for 3 minutes till fluffy and light. Put the egg and beat to blend. Put 1/3 cup of molasses and blend just to incorporate. Lower mixer speed to low and slowly put the dry ingredients; mix till blended. Gather dough together and wrap with plastic. Refrigerate for an hour till set.
- In upper and lower thirds of the oven, set the racks; preheat the oven to 350°F. Spoon out level tablespoonfuls of dough and roll among your hand palms making smooth rounds. Put on 2 baking sheets lined with parchment, set approximately 2-inch away, each sheet should accommodate approximately 12 rounds.
- Let the cookies bake for 9 to 12 minutes, rotating baking sheets top to bottom and back to front midway through, till just set around edges, bake less for chewier cookies, and bake a bit longer for crispier cookie. Allow the cookies to cool on baking sheets for 5 minutes, then put to wire racks and let cool fully.
- Redo with the rest of the dough, with new parchment paper on the baking sheets.
- In a medium bowl, mix remaining 1 tablespoon molasses, milk and powdered sugar till smooth. Glaze should be glossy and really thick yet remain pourable. If necessary, put additional water or milk half-teaspoonful at a time till right consistency is attained. Sprinkle the glaze on top of cookies and scatter raw sugar and additional pepper on top.
- Cookies can be glazed and baked 2 days in advance. When the glaze is firm, keep at room temperature airtight, or unglazed cookies can be freeze in resealable plastic bags up to a month.

Nutrition Information

- Calories: 276
- Protein: 3 g(5%)
- Total Fat: 8 g(13%)
- Saturated Fat: 5 g(25%)
- Sodium: 167 mg(7%)
- Fiber: 1 g(5%)
- Total Carbohydrate: 49 g(16%)
- Cholesterol: 36 mg(12%)

88. Sticky Sweet Grilled Pork Shoulder With Hoisin And Molasses

Serving: 8 servings | Prep: | Ready in:

Ingredients

- 2 heads of garlic, cloves separated, peeled
- 1 (wide, 6") piece ginger, peeled, chopped
- 1 cup hoisin sauce
- 3/4 cup fish sauce
- 2/3 cup honey
- 2/3 cup Shaoxing (Chinese rice) wine
- 1/2 cup chili oil
- 1/3 cup oyster sauce
- 1/3 cup toasted sesame oil
- 1 (4–5-lb.) skinless boneless pork shoulder (Boston butt)
- Kosher salt
- 3/4 cup (packed) dark brown sugar
- 1 Tbsp. mild-flavored (light)molasses
- Bread-and-butter pickles, white bread, cilantro, and rinsed thinly sliced white onion (for serving)

Direction

- Pork: Puree sesame oil, oyster sauce, chili oil, wine, honey, fish sauce, hoisin sauce, ginger and garlic till very smooth in a blender; for glaze, put 1 1/2 cups in a small bowl. Cover; chill till needed. Put leftover marinade in resealable 2-gal. plastic bag.
- Put pork shoulder on a cutting board, short end facing you, fat side down. Create shallow cut along whole length of long side of shoulder, holding long sharp knife 1-1 1/2-in. above cutting board. Keep cutting deeper into

meat, lifting then unfurling using your free hand, till it lies flat. It's best to get 2-3 even pieces rather than a single uneven piece. Put in bag with marinade; seal. Press air out. Work pork around the inside of bag to coat in marinade; chill for a minimum of 8 hours and up to 1 day.

- Prep Big Green Egg on medium heat; thermometer should read 350°F with cover closed. Take pork from marinade; let excess drip off. Season with salt all over lightly. Fit convection plate on grill; put pork over. Bank coals onto 1 side if you don't have convection plate; set pork on cooler area to prevent flare-ups. Cover; roast pork till an inserted instant-read thermometer in thickest part reads 140-145°F. You may do initial cooking in 350°F oven. Put on cutting board; rest for 20 minutes minimum.
- Assembly and glaze: Simmer reserved marinade, molasses and brown sugar in a big saucepan; cook for 6-8 minutes till reduced by 1/3 third to get 1 1/3 cups and keep warm.
- Prep Big green egg to medium high heat or use a conventional grill. Grill the pork for 6-8 minutes, turning using 2 pairs of tongs and basting every minute more or less, till warmed through, inserted instant-read thermometer in thickest part must read 130°F-145°F, lightly charred in spots and thickly coated in glaze; don't overcook. Put on a cutting board; against grain, slice to 1/4-in. thick. Serve with onion, cilantro, bread and pickles.
- You can roast pork 2 days ahead. Cool then cover; chill.

Nutrition Information

- Calories: 956
- Cholesterol: 137 mg(46%)
- Protein: 36 g(73%)
- Total Fat: 58 g(90%)
- Saturated Fat: 14 g(72%)
- Sodium: 3100 mg(129%)
- Fiber: 1 g(5%)
- Total Carbohydrate: 67 g(22%)

89. Stout Spice Cake With Lemon Glaze

Serving: Serves 4 | Prep: | Ready in:

Ingredients

- 3 1/2 cups all-purpose flour
- 3/4 teaspoon salt
- 1 1/2 teaspoons baking soda
- 1 1/2 teaspoons double-acting baking powder
- 1 tablespoon ground ginger
- 3/4 teaspoon cinnamon
- 1/4 teaspoon ground cloves
- 3/4 teaspoon aniseed, ground in an electric spice grinder
- 3/4 cup unsulfured molasses
- 1 1/2 sticks (3/4 cup) unsalted butter, melted and cooled slightly
- 3/4 cup firmly packed dark brown sugar
- a 12-ounce bottle of stout
- 2 large eggs, beaten lightly
- 3/4 cup milk
- 2 cups chopped pecans, toasted lightly
- 1 cup confectioners' sugar
- 3 1/2 tablespoons fresh lemon juice

Direction

- Preheat an oven to 350°F. Butter a glass 12×8×2-inch baking dish. Sift together the spices, baking powder, baking soda, salt and flour into a big bowl. Mix together the milk, eggs, stout, brown sugar, butter and molasses in a bowl and to flour mixture, put the mixture. Mix batter till incorporated and, mix in pecans. Batter will become thin. Into baking dish, put the batter, let the cake bake for 30 to 35 minutes in the center of the oven, or till a tester gets out clean, and on a rack, allow to cool fully in the dish. Onto the rack, turn the cake out.
- Mix together the lemon juice and confectioners' sugar in a small bowl, put glaze

on top of cake, and scatter using a metal spatula, allowing it to drip down the sides. Allow the cake to sit for half an hour, or till glaze is firm.

Nutrition Information

- Calories: 1648
- Protein: 22 g(44%)
- Total Fat: 79 g(121%)
- Saturated Fat: 27 g(135%)
- Sodium: 1146 mg(48%)
- Fiber: 9 g(35%)
- Total Carbohydrate: 217 g(72%)
- Cholesterol: 189 mg(63%)

90. Strawberries With Molasses Sour Cream Sauce

Serving: Serves 2 | Prep: | Ready in:

Ingredients

- 1/2 cup sour cream
- 1/2 teaspoon sugar
- 1/8 teaspoon vanilla extract
- 2 tablespoons unsulfured molasses
- 1 pint strawberries, hulled and, if large, halved

Direction

- Beat together 1 tablespoon molasses, vanilla, sugar and sour cream in a small bowl till smooth. Distribute strawberries among 2 bowls and put sour cream sauce on top. Sprinkle the rest of molasses on top of servings.

Nutrition Information

- Calories: 231
- Protein: 2 g(5%)
- Total Fat: 12 g(18%)
- Saturated Fat: 7 g(33%)
- Sodium: 36 mg(2%)
- Fiber: 4 g(14%)
- Total Carbohydrate: 31 g(10%)
- Cholesterol: 30 mg(10%)

91. Striped Bass With Swiss Chard, Chestnuts, And Pomegranate Vinaigrette

Serving: Makes 4 servings | Prep: | Ready in:

Ingredients

- 7 tablespoons olive oil, divided
- 4 5-ounce striped bass fillets
- 2 cups (packed) thinly sliced Swiss chard
- 1 cup peeled roasted chestnuts*, or jarred chestnuts, chopped
- 1/3 cup dry white wine
- 1/3 cup bottled clam juice
- 3 tablespoons pomegranate molasses**
- 1 tablespoon Sherry wine vinegar
- 1 teaspoon Dijon mustard
- 1 large shallot, minced

Direction

- In big nonstick skillet, heat 3 tablespoons of oil over moderately-high heat. Scatter pepper and salt on each side of fish fillets; put to the skillet and let cook for 3 minutes each side till golden. Put the fish to the platter; tent using foil to retain warmth. To the skillet, put clam juice, wine, chestnuts and chard; let cook for 3 minutes till chard is just wilted. Put the chard mixture on top of fish with a slotted spoon; tent using foil. In skillet, boil the juices for 3 minutes to slightly reduce. Take skillet off heat; put shallot, mustard, vinegar and pomegranate molasses. Gradually mix in leftover 4 tablespoons of oil. Put pepper and salt to season vinaigrette. Scoop on top of fish and serve.
- To prepare the fresh chestnuts, begin with glossy, heavy nuts with smooth, firm shells.

On a side of every shell, cut a small cross to vent while nuts roast and for easier peeling later on. In a shallow roasting pan, put the chestnuts; drizzle with water. Allow to roast for 25 to 20 minutes in 400°F oven. In towel, wrap the hot chestnuts and squeeze to crush the shells. Maintain the nuts wrapped for 5 minutes prior to taking the hard-outer shell off even the brown skin inside, being careful of burning your fingers. A pound of fresh chestnuts is equivalent to approximately 2 cups once shelled.

Nutrition Information

- Calories: 494
- Cholesterol: 113 mg(38%)
- Protein: 28 g(56%)
- Total Fat: 27 g(42%)
- Saturated Fat: 4 g(20%)
- Sodium: 285 mg(12%)
- Fiber: 1 g(4%)
- Total Carbohydrate: 31 g(10%)

92. Sweet And Spicy Chipotle Glazed Ribs

Serving: Makes 2 servings | Prep: | Ready in:

Ingredients

- 1 2-pound rack baby back pork ribs
- 1/4 cup canned chipotle chiles*
- 3/4 cup red currant jelly
- 5 tablespoons pomegranate molasses**
- 1/4 cup low-salt chicken broth
- 2 tablespoons olive oil
- 1/4 teaspoon ground allspice

Direction

- Set the oven to 350°F for preheating. Use a foil to line the rimmed baking sheet. Place the metal rack on the sheet. Season the ribs all over with salt and pepper and arrange them on the rack, meat side down.
- Press the chilies through a sieve into a heavy small saucepan, discarding the solids. Put all the remaining ingredients into the pan. Mix over medium heat until well-blended and the sauce starts to boil. Season the sauce with salt to taste. Reserve 1/2 cup of the sauce in a small bowl.
- Brush the ribs with 2 tbsp. of sauce from the pan. Flip the ribs over and brush the other side with another 2 tbsp. of sauce. Roast the ribs for 1 1/2 hours, brushing them with 2 tbsp. of sauce every 15 minutes until the ribs are very tender. Cut the rack into individual ribs. The ribs are best when served with the reserved sauce.

Nutrition Information

- Calories: 1623
- Cholesterol: 313 mg(104%)
- Protein: 88 g(175%)
- Total Fat: 88 g(135%)
- Saturated Fat: 28 g(141%)
- Sodium: 660 mg(28%)
- Fiber: 2 g(6%)
- Total Carbohydrate: 121 g(40%)

93. Three Nut Pie With Cranberries

Serving: Serves 8 | Prep: | Ready in:

Ingredients

- 1 Buttermilk Pie Crust Dough disk
- 1/2 cup coarsely chopped walnuts
- 1/2 cup coarsely chopped pecans
- 1/2 cup sliced almonds
- 3/4 cup firmly packed dark brown sugar
- 1/2 cup light corn syrup
- 1/4 cup plus 2 tablespoons (3/4 stick) unsalted butter, melted, room temperature
- 3 large eggs

- 2 tablespoons unsulfured (light) molasses
- 1 teaspoon vanilla extract
- 1/4 teaspoon salt
- 1 1/2 cups cranberries (about 6 ounces)

Direction

- Preheat an oven to 400°F. On slightly floured surface, unroll pie crust disk to 13-inch-diameter round, approximately 1/8-inch thick. Roll up dough on rolling pin, and turn onto glass pie plate of 9-inch diameter. Lightly pat into place. Trim crust edges, retaining 3/4-inch overhang. Fold overhang under the crust to make crust flush with edge of pie pan. Flute edges for a decorative border. Freeze crust for 15 minutes till set.
- With foil, line a pie crust, retaining 3-inch overhang. Fill the foil with pie weights or beans. Fold excess foil slowly over crust edges. Bake for 15 minutes till crust is set. Take off beans and foil and keep baking for 10 minutes till crust just starts to color, pricking using toothpick in case crust bubbles. Allow to cool. Keep oven temperature.
- In the meantime, on cookie sheet, mix almonds, pecans and chopped walnuts. Toast the nuts for 10 minutes till just golden. Allow to cool.
- In bowl, beat salt, vanilla extract, molasses, eggs, butter, light corn syrup and brown sugar to blend. Mix in cranberries and toasted nuts. In the prepped crust, put the filing. Bake for 45 minutes till middle of the filling is set. Allow the pie to cool fully.

Nutrition Information

- Calories: 473
- Total Carbohydrate: 61 g(20%)
- Cholesterol: 93 mg(31%)
- Protein: 8 g(16%)
- Total Fat: 24 g(37%)
- Saturated Fat: 7 g(37%)
- Sodium: 297 mg(12%)
- Fiber: 4 g(14%)

94. Treacle Farls

Serving: Makes 4 small loaves | Prep: | Ready in:

Ingredients

- 4 cups all purpose flour
- 1/4 cup sugar
- 1 teaspoon baking soda
- 1/2 teaspoon ground ginger
- 1/4 teaspoon salt
- 1/4 cup (1/2 stick) chilled unsalted butter, cut into pieces
- 1 3/4 cups (about) buttermilk
- 2 tablespoons dark molasses

Direction

- Preheat the oven to 425°F. Flour the heavy big baking sheet. In a big bowl, mix the initial 5 ingredients. Put the butter and massage in using fingertips till mixture is similar to a fine meal. In a medium bowl, mix dark molasses and 1 cup buttermilk to incorporate. Into the dry ingredients, mix the buttermilk mixture. Slowly mix in sufficient leftover buttermilk to create soft dough. On slightly floured area, knead just till dough gathers together. Form into 8-inch circle, approximately 1 1/2-inch high. Slice into 4-wedges. Put the wedges to prepped sheet, setting apart. Let bake for 30 minutes till deep golden brown. Allow to cool on racks.

Nutrition Information

- Calories: 678
- Total Carbohydrate: 121 g(40%)
- Cholesterol: 35 mg(12%)
- Protein: 17 g(33%)
- Total Fat: 14 g(21%)
- Saturated Fat: 8 g(40%)
- Sodium: 628 mg(26%)
- Fiber: 3 g(14%)

95. Vanilla Ice Cream And Ginger Molasses Cookie Sandwiches

Serving: Makes 6 Sandwiches | Prep: | Ready in:

Ingredients

- 2 cups all purpose flour
- 2 teaspoons baking soda
- 2 1/2 teaspoons ground ginger
- 1 teaspoon ground cinnamon
- 1 teaspoon ground cloves
- 1 teaspoon salt
- 1/2 cup (1 stick) unsalted butter, room temperature
- 1/4 cup vegetable shortening, room temperature
- 1 cup (packed) dark brown sugar
- 1 egg
- 1/4 cup unsulfured (light) molasses
- 1 tablespoon grated orange peel
- Sugar
- 1 pint vanilla ice cream, softened slightly
- 1/2 cup chopped drained stem ginger in syrup
- Fresh strawberries, hulled, sliced

Direction

- To make cookies: into medium bowl, sift the initial 6 ingredients. In a big bowl, mix brown sugar, shortening and butter. Whisk the butter mixture with electric mixer till fluffy. Put the peel, molasses and egg; whisk till incorporated. Put in the dry ingredients; stir just till blended. Place a cover; refrigerate for an hour.
- Preheat the oven to 350°F. Grease 2 baking sheets with butter. Put the sugar in a small bowl. Shape dough into a dozen even portions with damp hands; form portions into balls. Roll in sugar to cover. Turn onto prepped sheets, set 2 1/2-inch away. Allow to bake for 15 minutes till cookies are light golden and cracked on surface yet remain soft. Let cool on sheets for a minute. Turn onto racks; cool fully.
- To make sandwiches: in a medium bowl, put the ice cream. Mix in the ginger. Put to freezer for half an hour till nearly firm.
- On a work area, put 6 cookies flat side facing up. Place 1/3 cup of ice cream on top of each. From edge of the cookies, scatter to quarter-inch. Put another cookie on top of each. Push to adhere. Put in the freezer. Freeze for a minimum of 2 hours till firm. Can be done a day in advance. Wrap securely; retain frozen.
- On plates, set the sandwiches. Jazz up with berries, serve.

Nutrition Information

- Calories: 665
- Cholesterol: 87 mg(29%)
- Protein: 7 g(14%)
- Total Fat: 30 g(46%)
- Saturated Fat: 15 g(76%)
- Sodium: 486 mg(20%)
- Fiber: 2 g(9%)
- Total Carbohydrate: 94 g(31%)

96. Whipped Sweet Potatoes With Nutmeg And Lemon

Serving: Serves 12 | Prep: | Ready in:

Ingredients

- 5 pounds deep orange sweet potatoes (yams), peeled, cut into 2-inch pieces
- 1/2 cup (1 stick) butter, room temperature
- 3 tablespoons unsulfured molasses
- 2 teaspoons grated lemon peel
- 1 1/2 teaspoons ground nutmeg
- Salt and pepper
- Minced fresh parsley
- Grated lemon peel
- Ground nutmeg

Direction

- In a big pot of boiling salted water, cook the sweet potatoes for 15 minutes till soft. Drain thoroughly. Put to a big bowl and with processor or mixer, puree in batches. Put back to the pot. Add in 1 1/2 teaspoons nutmeg, 2 teaspoons lemon peel, molasses and butter. Put pepper and salt to season. Can be made a day in advance. Put cover and chill. Over moderate heat, mix potato mixture to reheat and slightly thicken.
- Put the potatoes to a serving bowl. Put nutmeg, lemon and parsley on top.

Nutrition Information

97. Whole Egg Molasses Buttercream

Serving: Makes 6 cups | Prep: 25mins | Ready in:

Ingredients

- 6 large eggs, room temperature
- 1 1/2 cups sugar
- 1/2 teaspoon salt
- 3 cups (6 sticks) unsalted butter, room temperature and very soft
- 1 teaspoon vanilla extract
- 4 tablespoons plus 1 teaspoon molasses

Direction

- Put 1 cup water to right below a simmer in a medium saucepan on medium low heat; mix salt, sugar and eggs in a stand mixer bowl using handheld whisk. Put bowl over saucepan without touching water; cook egg mixture till an instant-read thermometer reads 160°F, slightly thickened and lightened in color, constantly whisking. Take off heat; beat with stand mixer with whisk attachment at medium speed for 10 minutes till tripled in volume and fully cooled. 1-2 tbsp. at a time, add butter; beat well after each till incorporated fully. Add molasses and vanilla; beat till just combined on medium low speed.
- You can make and refrigerate buttercream up to 5 days ahead or freeze for up to 1 month. Using refrigerated buttercream; sit at room temperature for 2 hours minimum till soft; beat with stand mixer with paddle attachment till smooth at medium speed. 1 tsp. at a time, beat in a little amount of water if texture isn't smooth. Defrost: Put buttercream from freezer into fridge to thaw overnight. Follow instructions to use refrigerated buttercream.

Nutrition Information

- Calories: 306
- Sodium: 77 mg(3%)
- Total Carbohydrate: 17 g(6%)
- Cholesterol: 117 mg(39%)
- Protein: 2 g(4%)
- Total Fat: 26 g(41%)
- Saturated Fat: 16 g(82%)

98. Whole Wheat Bran Bread Risney Manning

Serving: Makes 1 loaf | Prep: | Ready in:

Ingredients

- 1 1/2 cups Miller wheat bran or wheat germ (available at natural foods stores and some supermarkets)
- 2 1/2 cups whole-wheat flour
- 1 teaspoon salt
- 1 1/2 teaspoons baking soda
- 1/4 cup firmly packed dark brown sugar
- 2 cups buttermilk
- 1/2 cup unsulfured molasses
- 1/2 cup raisins if desired

Direction

- Mix the brown sugar, baking soda, salt, flour and bran in a bowl. Mix together molasses and buttermilk in a separate bowl, mix into the flour mixture till batter is incorporated well, and mix in the raisins. In a slightly oiled 8×4×3-inch loaf pan, drop the batter, and bake for 1 hour to 1 hour and 10 minutes in the center of a preheated 350°F oven, till bread sounds hollow when patted. Allow the bread to cool for 15 minutes in pan on a rack, flip it onto rack, and allow to cool fully.

Nutrition Information

- Calories: 290
- Protein: 9 g(18%)
- Total Fat: 2 g(3%)
- Saturated Fat: 1 g(3%)
- Sodium: 364 mg(15%)
- Fiber: 9 g(36%)
- Total Carbohydrate: 67 g(22%)
- Cholesterol: 2 mg(1%)

99. Whole Wheat Bread Hayes

Serving: Makes 2 loaves | Prep: | Ready in:

Ingredients

- 2 cups warm water (105°-115°F.)
- 1/4-ounce package (2 1/2 teaspoons) active dry yeast
- 1/4 cup molasses
- 5 to 6 cups whole-wheat flour
- 2 tablespoons sugar
- 2 teaspoons salt
- 1/2 cup canola oil
- an egg wash made by beating 1 large egg white with 1 teaspoon water
- 3 tablespoons old-fashioned rolled oats for sprinkling loaves

Direction

- Mix together yeast and 1 3/4 cups warm water in a small bowl and allow to sit for 5 minutes till frothy. Beat together molasses and the leftover quarter cup warm water in a measuring cup. Mix together oil, salt, sugar and 2 cups flour in a big bowl and put the molasses and yeast mixtures, mixing till incorporated thoroughly. For mixture to create a soft dough, mix in sufficient of the leftover 3 to 4 cups flour, half-cup at a time, and transfer dough onto a slightly floured area. Knead the dough for 8 minutes, or till pliable and smooth, and form into a ball.
- To a slightly greased bowl, put the dough flipping to coat then cover in plastic wrap and allow to rise for 1 hour in a warm area till doubled in volume. Punch dough down and allow to rise with cover for 45 minutes longer.
- Preheat the oven to 400°F. Oil two 8 1/2×4 1/2×2-inch loaf pans.
- Split dough in half. Gently knead every dough piece and shape into ovals. Put the loaves to pans, cover using kitchen towels and allow to rise for 45 minutes. Slightly glaze tops of loaves with egg wash and scatter oats over. Let loaves bake in center of the oven for 10 minutes. Lower the oven temperature to 350°F. Allow the loaves to bake for 20 to 25 minutes longer, or till golden brown. Transfer loaves onto a rack to let cool.

Nutrition Information

- Calories: 304
- Saturated Fat: 1 g(5%)
- Sodium: 273 mg(11%)
- Fiber: 6 g(25%)
- Total Carbohydrate: 48 g(16%)
- Protein: 8 g(16%)
- Total Fat: 11 g(16%)

100. Winterfell Black Bread

Serving: Makes 1 loaf | Prep: | Ready in:

Ingredients

- 2/3 cup warm water
- 1 3/4 teaspoons active dry yeast (1 package)
- 3 tablespoons molasses
- 2 teaspoons canola oil
- 1 cup medium rye flour
- 1 teaspoon kosher salt
- 1 tablespoon caraway seeds, toasted and ground
- 2-3 cups bread flour
- 1 tablespoon honey
- 1 tablespoon strong coffee

Direction

- Mix 1 tablespoon of molasses, yeast and water in a big bowl. Mix to dissolve and allow to sit for 10 minutes till frothy.
- Put in the rye flour, oil and leftover molasses; mix to incorporate. Put caraway, salt and sufficient bread flour to form a stiff dough. Put flour only to lessen the stickiness. Transfer onto a floured area and knead for 5 to 8 minutes. Put back to bowl, dust surface with the flour, and cover using a plastic wrap or wet cloth. Let rise at room temperature for 2 hours till doubled in size.
- With pan spray, grease a 9×5-inch loaf pan and with a strip of parchment, line the base and short sides. In case pan spray and parchment are not available, instead oil the sides and base of pan with vegetable shortening. Onto a floured area, transfer risen dough and form into an oblong loaf. Put into prepped pan and reserve to proof for half an hour, or till dough rises on top of the pan. Preheat the oven to 350°F.
- Mix coffee and honey; onto the top of risen dough, brush softly. Let bake for 30-40 minutes till empty sounding and golden brown. Allow to cool for 10 minutes, take off from pan, and let cool fully on a rack.

Nutrition Information

- Calories: 256
- Total Fat: 3 g(4%)
- Saturated Fat: 0 g(1%)
- Sodium: 218 mg(9%)
- Fiber: 4 g(16%)
- Total Carbohydrate: 51 g(17%)
- Protein: 9 g(17%)

101. Yankee Oatmeal Molasses Bread

Serving: Makes 1 loaf | Prep: | Ready in:

Ingredients

- 1/2 cup packed old-fashioned oats
- 3/4 cup boiling water
- 1 cup warm water (105°F to 115°F)
- 1 envelope dry yeast
- 6 tablespoons lightly unsulfured molasses
- 2 tablespoons (1/4 stick) butter, room temperature
- 1 1/4 teaspoons salt
- 4 1/2 cups (about) unbleached all purpose flour
- 1 tablespoon melted butter mixed with 1 teaspoon light unsulfured molasses (glaze)
- 1 tablespoon old-fashioned oats

Direction

- In a big bowl of an electric mixer with dough hook attachment, put half cup of oats; put 3/4 cup of boiling water on top. Allow to sit for half an hour, till water is soaked in and oatmeal is really soft.
- Into glass 2-cup measuring cup, put a cup of warm water. Scatter the yeast on surface; mix to incorporate. Allow to sit for 10 minutes till yeast dissolves. Into the oat mixture in a bowl, combine salt, 2 tablespoons butter and molasses. Add in the yeast mixture. Put sufficient flour, a cup at a time, to create a moderately-soft dough, combining at moderate speed till well incorporated for 3 minutes. Transfer the dough onto a floured

- area. Knead till pliable and smooth for 5 minutes, putting additional flour in case dough is very sticky. Shape the dough into round. Grease a big bowl with butter; put the dough, flipping to coat. Using plastic wrap, cover the bowl, then the towel. Allow the dough to rise in warm draft-free place for an hour till doubled in size.
- In middle of the oven, place the rack and preheat the oven to 400°F. Butter a loaf pan, 9x5-inch in size. Punch dough down; transfer into a floured area and knead for 3 minutes. Shape into 8-inch-long loaf. Put to prepped pan. Cover using plastic, then the towel; allow to rise in warm draft-free place for 45 minutes till dough has risen approximately half-inch above rim of pan.
- Let the bread bake for 10 minutes; lower the temperature to 350°F. Allow to bake for 25 minutes more. With glaze, brush the surface of bread; scatter 1 tablespoon oats on top. Allow to bake for 10 minutes more till bread sounds empty once tapped on bottom and turn golden. Put to rack; let cool for 10 minutes in pan. Transfer bread onto rack; cool fully. Can be prepared 2 weeks in advance. Wrap securely in foil and put in freezer. In 350°F oven rewarm wrapped bread about 15 minutes if wished.

Nutrition Information

- Calories: 285
- Cholesterol: 6 mg(2%)
- Protein: 7 g(13%)
- Total Fat: 3 g(5%)
- Saturated Fat: 2 g(8%)
- Sodium: 279 mg(12%)
- Fiber: 2 g(9%)
- Total Carbohydrate: 57 g(19%)

Index

A
Apple 3,4,6,7,20,55
Apricot 3,36

B
Bacon 3,9,10,45
Baking 49
Beans 3,12
Beef 3,12
Blueberry 3,13,39,40
Bran 4,58,67
Bread 3,4,15,34,36,42,50,54,61,67,68,69
Broth 5
Butter 3,4,6,10,25,26,27,29,30,35,39,46,49,52,55,62,64,67,70

C
Cake 3,4,6,7,19,23,25,27,28,29,33,36,51,55,62
Caramel 3,30
Carrot 4,56
Chard 4,63
Cheese 3,28
Cherry 3,17
Chestnut 4,63
Chicken 3,11,14
Chipotle 3,4,17,31,64
Chocolate 3,17
Coffee 3,19
Cognac 52
Cream 3,4,6,14,19,23,28,30,35,42,49,52,54,58,63,66
Crisps 3,46

Cumin 3,4,22,52

D
Date 3,24
Dijon mustard 11,33,63
Dill 1,2
Duck 3,47

E
Egg 3,4,22,62,67

F
Fat 3,6,7,8,9,10,11,12,14,15,16,17,19,20,21,22,23,24,25,26,27,28,29,30,31,32,33,34,35,36,37,40,41,42,43,44,45,46,47,48,49,50,51,52,53,54,55,56,57,58,59,60,61,62,63,64,65,66,67,68,69,70
Flour 49,65
Fruit 3,19

G
Giblets 5
Gin 3,4,6,9,10,13,16,19,21,23,24,25,26,27,28,29,30,31,33,36,37,39,43,44,46,49,51,52,53,54,55,57,66
Gravy 3,44,45

H
Ham 3,32
Honey 3,23

I
Ice cream 35
Icing 3,46

J
Jus 16,47

L
Lamb 3,38

Lemon 3,4,38,39,40,62,66

Lime 3,41

M

Marmalade 4,55

Milk 3,34,43

Mince 5,66

Molasses 1,3,4,5,10,12,14,16,17,22,24,25,31,32,34,38,41,42,43,44,45,46,49,50,53,56,57,60,61,63,66,67,69

Muffins 3,4,24,48,58

Mustard 3,32

N

Nut 3,4,5,6,7,8,9,10,11,12,13,14,15,16,17,19,20,21,22,23,24,25,26,27,28,29,30,31,32,33,34,35,36,37,38,39,40,41,42,43,44,45,46,47,48,49,50,51,52,53,54,55,56,57,58,59,60,61,62,63,64,65,66,67,68,69,70

O

Oatmeal 3,4,48,69

Oil 20,34,37,42,49,50,68

Onion 3,43

Orange 3,19,31,50

P

Pancakes 3,13

Paprika 5

Pecan 3,17

Peel 18,40

Perry 3,20

Pie 3,4,17,38,39,60,64

Pineapple 4,51

Pistachio 3,28,29

Pomegranate 3,4,22,47,52,63

Pork 3,4,32,45,61

Potato 4,66

Prune 3,4,48,52

Pumpkin 3,4,24,51,53,60

R

Rum 3,32,43

S

Salad 3,4,8,57

Salt 5,11,66

Sausage 3,10

Seeds 3,5

Sherry 4,56,57,63

Soda 3,42

Soup 3,11

Steak 4,50

Stock 44

Stuffing 5

Sugar 26,66

Swiss chard 63

T

Tabasco 11,50

Turkey 3,5,44

V

Vinegar 4,56

W

Wine 3,47

Worcestershire sauce 11,12,14,17,44,45

Y

Yam 3,10

Conclusion

Thank you again for downloading this book!

I hope you enjoyed reading about my book!

If you enjoyed this book, please take the time to share your thoughts and post a review on Amazon. It'd be greatly appreciated!

Write me an honest review about the book – I truly value your opinion and thoughts and I will incorporate them into my next book, which is already underway.

Thank you!

If you have any questions, **feel free to contact at:** *author@rutabagarecipes.com*

Kelly Dill

rutabagarecipes.com

CPSIA information can be obtained
at www.ICGtesting.com
Printed in the USA
BVHW020955200323
660786BV00008B/83